How to Publish the Damn Book

Other Books by E. Prybylski

Boston Blight

Smoke & Magic

- Fallen
- Hot & Cold

Frost & Shadow

- Cold Front

How to Finish the Damn Book

- How to Write the Damn Book
- How to Publish the Damn Book

Short Story Collections

- When Nightmares Fall — Edited by Elizabeth Harvey
- Damn Faeries — Edited by Elizabeth Harvey
- Invisible, Not Imagined — Edited by Rock and Roll Saved My Soul
- Fields of Broken Steel — Edited by M. Ngai
- Daughter of Spring — Edited by N.D. Gray
- Scion of Summer — Edited by N.D. Gray
- Heir of Autumn — Edited by N.D. Gray
- Ink Stained and Spellbound — Edited by N.D. Gray
- Sister Death — Edited by N.D. Gray
- Halls of Ghostly Holly — Edited by N.D. Gray

HOW TO PUBLISH THE DAMN BOOK

A guide to becoming a damn author

Ellis Prybylski

*ISBN Print: 9798987571965
ISBN Ebook: 9798987571972*

Contents

Chapter Eleven —— 149
Marketing Principles

Chapter Twelve —— 167
Finding Your Target Audience

Chapter Thirteen —— 185
Social Media for Authors

Chapter Fourteen — 196
Advertising

Chapter Fifteen —— 214
Author Events

Introduction

Hello, friend! I am Ellis Prybylski (a.k.a. E. Prybylski) and have been in the publishing industry as a professional since 2008. I am of Celtic descent and a non-binary trans person, autistic, and have ADHD. I'm leading with those things because if any of those elements shock or dismay you, I am not likely someone you want to spend your time with.

I am the head of Insomnia Self-Publishing Services and the head administrator of the Neurodivergent Publishing Conference. At the time of writing this, I serve as the New England chapter head for the Editorial Freelancers Association and am working with Author Nation to develop their New England presence as well. I share these things not to tell you how important I am, but to give you an idea of where my experience and credentials lie when I talk about publishing.

Please feel free to contact me if you have questions this book doesn't answer. Send me a message, and I'll gladly help where I can or guide you to my coaching services if it's a question we can't answer quickly together.

In addition to the above things, I am an author, a tabletop role-playing game nerd, a musician, a historian and reenactor (Society for Creative Anachronism), a martial artist and fencer, and a gamer. Honestly, I'm never sure what to put into these things. My social media is mostly photos of my cats, bad jokes, and writing advice. I am nothing if not a collection of weird hobbies in a trench coat.

At the end of the day, I'm just a human being meandering my way through life just like you are. I have experience that I think could be useful to others, and after repeating the advice in this book so many times I feel like I could write it in my sleep, I decided to put this work together.

So what is this book for? It's to act as a guide. Publishing is a big world, and there are so many moving parts that figuring out where the hell to start can feel like an impossible task. Particularly for neurodivergent folks like myself, though it can be true for anybody.

In the rest of these pages, you will find the distillation of my sixteen years (at time of writing) of industry experience. Throughout my career, I have worked for traditional publishers, owned a traditional publishing company myself, and worked extensively with indie authors. I don't believe in smoke in mirrors, and there is no "secret sauce." What's in these pages are lessons you could learn on your own if you spent sixteen years studying the industry like I have.

I am not the only expert on this material, and I highly encourage you to read more than one book on the subject of writing and publishing. Take whatever of this works for you and leave what doesn't. What works for one person may not work for another, but I have done my absolute best to put the most evergreen, useful advice I have into this work.

What this book represents is a way for you to develop your publishing *strategy*. Tactics will change. Specific outlets will come and go as social media changes. However, strategy is a broader, deeper thing based on longer-term principles and ideas. The landscape of publishing can and will change. I've witnessed incredible revolutions taking place in the sphere, and I am friends with people who've been in "the biz" for fifty years or more and have seen yet more changes than I have. Those changes, however, do not delete the principles I share in this book. If you understand nothing else, please take away the underpinnings of *why* I share this information. I do everything I can to give you as much insight into my reasons as possible, and that is going to provide you more mileage than the specific tactics that may come and go overnight as technology advances and as new platforms and methods grow, bloom, and die.

Chapter One

What It Means to Be an Author

Choosing to be an author versus a writer is one of those decisions you should spend some time sitting with. It's a choice that will affect your life for a long time and comes with a lot of other elements that you may or may not have considered. This chapter is going to discuss the elements of being an author and what comes along with it in an attempt to help you decide if this is really for you.

I want to be very clear about the fact that if this isn't for you, there is no shame in that. You are allowed to write for fun and share it for free on various platforms to connect with others. Publishing professionally is a completely different animal than writing for fun, and we need to acknowledge that elephant in the room. In fact, publishing professionally is not for everyone. You can be just as valid and wonderful a writer without ever publishing for money, and I don't want anyone to think they either need to do this or quit writing.

We live in a culture that doesn't appreciate people doing art for art's sake, and that reality drives a lot of people to turn hobbies they're passionate about into businesses they end up hating. I don't want that for you. If you are choosing to be an author, I want you to do it with your eyes open and full awareness of what that will mean for you.

All that said, being an author is rewarding, exciting, and wonderful. I wouldn't trade it for the world. My intent here is not to in any way make you feel like you're going to fail at it. In fact, this whole book is dedicated to trying to help you succeed in every way I know how.

Accepting the Business Side of Writing

One of the first things to address in this whole book is the fact that, when we choose to publish—from the minute we start taking that seriously and regarding it as more than a pipe dream—we have to consider the realities of writing *as a business*.

This means that, while we are of course artists in our own right, we have to become more than that pretty quickly. For those who are not prepared for this, the need to view their work as a business proposition is often an unpleasant surprise.

If you've bought this book, I presume you already know that writing a book is more than drafting something and then slapping it up on Amazon with a cover you made in Microsoft Paint. And if you didn't know that before, you definitely do now! The business of book publishing is complex and specific and requires industry knowledge in order to be successful.

In many ways, it's very similar to operating any small business: You have to make decisions about your finances, your work, your ROI, your costs, and come to a conclusion about the best possible choice for you. As such, please recognize that my advice here isn't one size fits all. While I can provide principles, information, and ideas, you may have needs not addressed in this book. Some of my recommendations may also not fit your unique situation.

Should you be in a situation where none of my advice feels right, you can absolutely hire a large variety of professionals to coach you through making the decisions you need to make. There are also a huge number of writing organizations out there with people whose brains you can pick. Of course, some are more trustworthy and knowledgeable than others, so *caveat emptor*.

When I talk about accepting the business side of writing, however, what I mean is knowing that you have to step outside the bounds of writing for fun. When writing becomes a business, it comes with challenges and pressures that differ from choices about your manuscript. While writing, you are focused on the art, but when you start considering publication, you must look at your work and writing with new eyes: as a product on a shelf.

We're going to go through this step by step together and talk over what that entails. For now, however, take a moment and sit with that reality. From here on out, we are talking about your book as we would any product on a store shelf. That means it's not your brainchild so much as it is something you are trying to sell to others.

This mentality is going to help you in the long run with making assessments for your business. If you don't have some of that degree of separation from your work when making these decisions, you will fall into traps. I am not, of course, suggesting that you stop caring about your work, your characters, your world, or your artistic integrity. Far from it. However, we need to care about them *differently* and view them through the lens of: How do I make this product worth the money people are going to invest in it?

Whether you are publishing traditionally or on your own, you are asking people to invest in the product *and in you*. Whether it's investing the money to produce the book (which is not a small amount of money) or whether it's the cost of purchasing the book or even the costs of doing business, these are all financial decisions and must be made with a business eye.

Becoming a Small Business Owner

I went to business school for several years before transitioning my degree over into history, so this concept fit me better than it fits many authors who see writing as a hobby they might make money at. However, much as we need to accept that publishing books means we need to see our writing through business eyes, it also means we need to see *ourselves* through business eyes.

As soon as you publish a book, you are no longer just a private citizen. You can, and should, keep elements of your life private, but publishing a book means that you, or a persona you create for a pen name, become a public figure.

You become a business owner. And the product you're selling is, ultimately, yourself.

I'm not suggesting you necessarily go out and file paperwork to become an LLC, though it's a good option if you intend to self-publish because it provides certain legal protections. The mental exercise of considering yourself as a businessperson is more about capturing that mindset more than it is the brass tacks of business ownership. That said, you really should keep track of the things you purchase for your author work because they count as business expenses on your taxes. I'm not an accountant, so I'm not going to give you specific financial advice on that score, but it's something to keep in mind.

Viewing all the decisions you're going to need to make for your book as business and financial decisions—from choosing whether to self-publish or traditional or hybrid— will help some with the overwhelm, too. If you are feeling like this is all too much and too frightening and want to hide in a hole somewhere, that's okay. The good thing is business decisions can be broken down into pros and cons; they are finite, and they are specific.

It's not an ephemeral "business, business, business, numbers (is this working?)" situation. There's a concrete, logical flow you can use to make these assessments, and feeling like you've got a handle on it will come from two sources: experience and knowledge. If you don't have experience yet—which I suspect you don't, if you're reading this book—you will gain knowledge. When you understand the decision you need to make, and you know the impact it will have on you and on your goals, it becomes far easier to make the decision.

The Role of Marketing

I'm going to bust this myth again later in the book, but let me state here right in the beginning: *Whether you publish traditionally or on your own, you will be responsible for your marketing.* Traditional publishers will support your marketing efforts, amplify your voice, and put money toward advertising, but they are not going to do all your marketing. That old chestnut has been floating around at least since I started in the publishing world sixteen years ago. It's probably been around longer than that, if I'm honest, and it's *never* been true. I've had conversations with bestselling authors who started publishing before I was born. They had to buy books, load them into a wagon, and sell them door-to-door to bookstores.

There will be a lot on marketing in the scope of this guide, but for the purposes of beginning the conversation about it, let's think about what marketing is and isn't.

Marketing is, in essence, any action you take that helps other people know you've written a book. That's it. Anything you do to let people know you've written a book or are an author is marketing. It's a broad category of activities all together under a single umbrella. While the concept of it usually terrifies creatives, it's a lot less horrible than we think if we break it down into bite-sized pieces.

In book publishing, the role of marketing is to sell your books. Nobody on the planet is going to sell your books in a vacuum. Even if you hire a publicist or are lucky enough to have one assigned to you, you are going to need to take actions to engage with fans, raise visibility, and tell people about your work. A publicist might book events, create social media content, and find ways to get eyes on you, but you're not going to be out of the spotlight. You are still going to have to do the work, too. A publicist just takes certain elements of that work off your plate.

Knowing When You're Ready to Publish

The first question you need to ask yourself in this whole process is this: "Is my book ready?" Knowing the answer to that will give you valuable insight into where you are in the scope of things and what steps you need to take at the current time to achieve your goal of publishing your book.

Answering this question is pretty simple, and it can be found in the format of the first book of this series. Did you take the steps outlined in that book?

Have you:

- Finished writing the book?
- Self-edited the book to the best of your ability?

- Sent the book to beta readers and revised based on their feedback?

If the answer to all those questions is *yes*, then you're ready to prepare for the process of publishing it. If the answer to any of those questions is *no*, then I suggest pumping the brakes and finishing whatever elements you haven't yet. Your book doesn't need to be *perfect* before starting the publication process—particularly since you'll likely be working with a professional editor at some point—but it needs to be as good as you can get it.

This might get me some flak from people who despise prescriptive advice, and I've been called a "gatekeeper" before because I have strong opinions on this matter. However, I'm going to tell you this anyway because I believe it is extremely important information for you to have: *Your first completed manuscript of your life is unlikely to be publishable when you finish it.*

This isn't to say your first story is not something you should keep, but in no other industry do people think your first produced work is something worth selling. For visual artists, nobody thinks the first stick figure they put together should go up for sale on Etsy. For musicians, the first song they ever wrote probably isn't going up on Spotify. The same is true for authors. If you have never finished a manuscript before in your life, and you have no significant experience in writing, you should take some time and really study the craft before charging onward to publication.

Writers seem to have this unique pressure to sell their work immediately, or this idea that their first works are saleable. I think perhaps it's because we are taught the language as children, so we don't view writing as a separate skill from what we're taught in school. We think that, since we learned how to write and use language, we must be prepared to use those skills to write books. Unfortunately, that just isn't the case. Story craft is a skill unto itself and has separate rules from essay writing. Even then, doing something for fun is an entirely different category for doing it for money.

Pen Names and Their Role

Writing under a sobriquet is as old as the craft of writing itself. People have used pen names to obscure their identity since time immemorial, and having a pen name is one of those things many people want because the idea of being known as their real name on a public stage is terrifying.

There is nothing wrong with using a pen name, but there are a few things you will need to know about it as far as brass tacks things go, and if you are considering using multiple pen names, things become even more complicated. To be entirely honest, I suggest against multiple pen names unless you absolutely need them. I'll get into when you might want to split your writing into multiple pen names later, but for now, let's talk about a few things that apply to all pen names.

Also, since this has been a thing that has happened before: If you create a persona around this pen name, please do not appropriate other cultures or portray yourself as someone you are not. You can have a pen name that's a different gender, but stick to your own identities if you are constructing one for your pen name.

There have been a number of authors who have created pen names as people of color, people of gender identities they don't have—minority ones, not majority ones—and who portrayed themselves as someone they absolutely are not. Please use care when selecting your pen name and identity because this kind of thing ends careers.

You will need to do business under your legal name.

This means when you make purchases, sign documents, or receive money, you must do so under your legal name. *You can't sign on with a publisher as an anonymous person without using your legal name because they absolutely need it.* They may also require your social security number (SSN) for tax purposes and to send you tax paperwork, depending on how your publisher operates. When you set yourself up to distribute books through Amazon or any other platform, they will require an Employer

Identification Number (EIN) or SSN. There's no avoiding it.

Your pen name is your brand.

Even with a pen name, you will need to share some elements of yourself. Even if those elements are very limited, you cannot be entirely "faceless." I put that in quotation marks because I don't mean you need to share images of your face, but your brand will have to be identifiable. Whether you show photos of yourself or just use a logo or image, you'll need to have things people associate with you.

You shouldn't change your pen name without serious thought.

As with the last one, your brand is your identity. If people don't associate your name on the book with what they're looking for, they won't find you. If you develop a fan base under Bob Wrinkleshanks and decide to change over to Rob Smoothbottom, people won't know it's you and won't be able to find your books. Changing your pen name is as serious as a larger company trying to change its branding.

With all those things said, pen names are useful for keeping all of you out of the public eye. If you write certain genres, often erotica or romance), you might want to consider one unless you want everyone at the PTA meeting giving you the stare down. If you're okay with that, carry on. Also, historically, female writers in certain genres tended toward pen names that were more masculine because there are fools out there who don't believe women can write certain genres.

I don't believe that is as much of a problem these days, but it is a consideration in certain spheres. I choose to write under E. Prybylski because it's gender neutral, and my legal name is long and hard to fit on a book cover. I'm not hiding anything—I'm easy to find—but that's another reason you might consider writing under a name that isn't your given one.

Should I have multiple pen names?

Man, this is a hard question. There are many ways to approach this one, too. On one hand, if you write in multiple genres, it can help tell readers what you're writing (e.g., Nora Roberts versus J.D. Robb). However, Nora Roberts has not tried to hide her connection to her J.D. Robb pen name and just uses it to identify the crime novels she writes versus her sweet romance. As you can see, those are two disparate markets, and as such, she needs to differentiate.

If you write in a genre that you don't want to bleed over into your other books, having multiple pen names makes sense. I know folks who write furry novels. There's not a lot of acceptance of furries in the world, sadly, so keeping the furry writing separated by a pen name makes perfect sense.

This does, however, create a branding issue.

Unless you're doing what Nora Roberts does, multiple pen names means multiple brands. It also means marketing to multiple, separate audiences. If you have limited time and means, that can be a real pain in the backside, if I'm honest. It might mean managing multiple social media accounts that cannot cross streams, and it means you have to build your readership up from absolute zero when you start a new one.

Is this impossible? No, of course not. It's very doable, but it requires compartmentalization and time. If there's one thing I know about authors, it's that we often don't have a lot of time as it is because we're trying to balance our writing careers with day jobs, families, and life in general.

As usual, the answer to this question comes down to what works for you. Can you manage multiple brands? Do you need to? Is it something that is necessary for your writing? If you can answer *yes* to those questions, then by all means. But if you're unsure if you can keep those plates spinning, it may be better to find a way to stay under one brand or stick the other works on the shelf until you're ready to step into the space of managing multiple.

Summary

Through this chapter we discussed the realities of what it means to be an author who is publishing their work for profit. It's a different world than just writing for the sake of writing and demands we reconsider our relationship to our writing as we step into the realm of business. Cultivating the ability to think of things in terms of cost and benefit and so on is necessary in order to be successful at publishing.

Key Takeaways

- The decision to become an author whose books people purchase means reevaluating your manuscript from the position of "how do I sell this."

- Choosing to publish means essentially either becoming a small business owner, yourself (self-publishing) or partnering with a publisher in a business venture. Knowing how to view things through this lens is a vital skill and will adjust your approach to selling books and selling yourself.

- Marketing is a vital part of publishing successfully and cannot be avoided.

- There are some clear indicators of when you are ready to publish your book. If you aren't ready to publish it, that's okay, but make sure you don't publish before it's ready.

- Having a pen name is an option but not a necessity. It requires consideration and should be approached with careful thought.

Chapter Two

How to Think Like a Businessperson

As we have begun to do, thinking like a businessperson is key to the success of your works as an author. Knowing when to wear your "business hat" versus your "writer hat" will get you a lot farther than you think. Most authors are creatives by nature, and thinking like a businessperson will feel foreign and uncomfortable. It requires us to be more mercenary than we may be comfortable with, and it demands a different kind of thought from us.

The core fundamentals of business and how to make those decisions are something a lot of authors come into this without the experience of doing. Many of us flounder as a result, so making those decisions and learning how to shift gears will be of utmost importance to your career as a whole. Having run a business for many years and having studied it on a collegiate level, I can say with certainty that this knowledge is going to differentiate successful authors from those who flounder about in the margins.

That isn't to say this is some silver bullet or magic potion. It isn't. These principles and this understanding still have to be put into practice, and it takes time and study to perfect. Be patient with yourself as you learn.

Making Business Decisions

Going from the creator mindset to the business mindset is hard. They involve completely different decisions and come from different parts of the brain. That's not to say that marketing isn't creative—it is. However, it's a different kind of creativity than you might think. The same goes with business choices.

When we start viewing our writing as a business, we need to evaluate things like ROI (return on investment) and cost-benefit analysis. We need to start keeping track of expenditures for the purposes of taxes. We need to do so much more than think about our plot and characters, and it's often overwhelming because we aren't accustomed to that.

Small business owners live this, and if you have that experience, you'll understand what I'm getting at here. Making choices based on business sense is its own skill. In this chapter, I'm going to explain some of these terms and how to make these choices.

Thinking in terms of business is a combination of things that seem like they're basic, simple logic, and things that feel like they're too complicated, so we don't wanna. Just recognize that this takes practice and time, and it means putting your work at arm's length and making choices based on things more solid than our feelings. We love our books and have strong feelings about them, but when it comes to asking people to give us money for something, that's where the rubber meets the road.

This is also where traditional publishing sometimes can be a boon. Other than choosing which publisher to go with and doing some of the marketing, the publisher handles the business decisions for you. If you don't think you're cut out for that kind of thing, looking for a traditional publisher might be a way to avoid having to learn these things, or at least as many of them anyhow.

Cost-Benefit Analysis

Cost-benefit analysis is the cornerstone of business thought. What it means, in essence, is that you need to look at how much something will cost versus what benefit you will reap. We make these decisions all the time and every day; we just usually don't frame them that way. Decisions like whether or not you want to buy the next game in a franchise when the last one didn't wow you is a cost-benefit analysis.

When looking at publishing, these choices will look like: whether to go indie or trad., whether to hire an editor or not, whether a certain kind of advertising is worth the money. Those are the sorts of decisions you'll have to make financially, and they're the kind of decisions that will shape your writing career.

This kind of thought *also* has an impact on your craft. The choice of whether or not to write to market, for example. If you don't know what that means, it means analyzing current trends and fads in the book world and writing a book that capitalizes on them. Writing to market might well mean you make more money, but if that's not where your heart is, it may be a cost of your own enjoyment of the process. I say *may* because if you enjoy writing the kind of content that's "in" right now, you could end up in the sweet spot. I will be discussing some of these things later on, so don't get too hung up on that specific example yet.

So how do we do a cost-benefit analysis?

Performing a cost-benefit analysis is pretty straightforward. Essentially, you draw up a list of pros and cons, including the cost and the potential rewards. You consider risks and think about what the consequences of those risks might be. Then you make a decision.

For myself, I tend to default to doing this on paper with a pen because I'm a fuddy duddy. But there are many methods. Usually, I will write four columns whose names I've already identified: Pros, Cons, Risks, and Rewards. Then you start filling them in.

- Example: Should I add sex to my urban fantasy series?
- Pros: Sex sells; might capture a part of the market I don't have.
- Cons: My publisher doesn't publish spicy

books, so I'd need to self-publish; I'm not sure this book series really needs it; I don't want to force sex in because it's popular.

- Risks: Not having sex on the page of my books will cut out a certain segment of the market.

- Rewards: I'd get to stay with my publisher; my book series will stay true to what I'd planned for it

This list is simplistic, and they can absolutely be larger and more complex and might need to be, depending on the decisions you're trying to make. That said, it's a good example of how to work through the process.

This is an actual thought process I had, too. Whether or not I wanted to add on-page sex to my urban fantasy series was a real thought process for me because, as it says under pros, sex sells. I just never planned mine to have it. After a lot of thought, I ended up deciding to have some on-page spicy scenes in my novels because they're important to the character development and demonstrate certain emotions. They're few and far between, but it's about the characters and their connection, not the sex.

You can do an analysis like this for almost any question you come across in your writing or your life. Using a method similar to the above will help you lay out all the pieces so you can see all the various options and pieces.

Questions to Ask

While considering the various pieces and parts of this exercise, you may be thinking you aren't sure what all the risks and rewards and such are. So here are a few questions you can ask to tease out these answers:

- If I do this, what's the best that could happen?

- If I do this, what's the worst that could happen?

- If I don't do this, what's the worst that could happen?

- If I don't do this, what's the best that could happen?

- How much will this thing cost me in money?
- How much will this thing cost me in time?
- How much will this thing save me in time in the long run?
- How much will this thing save me in money in the long run?
- Is it something that I will be able to sustain?
- How much money will this earn me if I am successful?
- How much will this thing cost me if I am not successful?
- Are there any alternatives I have not considered?
- Will this impact me financially in a way that will be a struggle to recoup?

Financial Considerations

Part of entering into the business space is understanding that this is going to impact your finances in more ways than just our hope that we can buy a mansion somewhere in Maine near Stephen King's. Choosing what method you want to take to publish your book is going to have a direct and significant impact in how much it will cost you. I'm going to dig deeper into the different publication methods in the next chapter, but I want to start you thinking about finances now.

Publishing a book well is not cheap. It just isn't. To do it utilizing the same techniques the Big Five employ (I'll get into cost cutting later), it will cost you *up to ten thousand dollars*. Before you choke on your tongue, you can bring this number down substantially as an indie author. However, it will *still* be an investment because if you are treating your writing like a business, you need to consider your overhead.

If you don't know the term, "overhead" is the things you need to pay for in order to do business. For a bakery, it would be things like rent, electricity, ingredients, employee wages, insurance, FDA licensing, internet, and so on. All these things are necessary elements of doing business. While you can absolutely cut corners, you can only cut so far before you really damage your end product which will, in turn, hurt your sales.

In the past, I have been told I am "gatekeeping" when I bring this up, but it's no more gatekeeping than telling a baker that if they use chalk dust instead of flour, it might be cheaper but will devastate their sales. While books aren't likely to cause anybody gastrointestinal distress or kill them, if publishing is a business, it has overhead.

The reason I mention this is because, if you're looking to be an author, you need to be prepared to invest in your book. There's no way around it. Whether you throw money at it or invest a great deal of time rather than solely hiring other people to do work for you, which is one of the cost cutting measures, you are still investing in it. Investing isn't just about cash assets, it's about equity. Value.

If the idea of spending money on publishing sounds discouraging, recognize that, if you go the traditional publishing route (indie or Big 5), you will need to spend dramatically less money on publishing your book. Being broke doesn't mean you can never publish your books and that you're locked out of the industry forever. It just means you may need to consider how you go about publishing them. The cost of publishing a book *well* is significant, and that's one of the main reasons why traditional publishers still exist.

I am, however, getting ahead of myself.

When looking at publishing, there are about a million things that will scream at you to give them money. There are book promoters, cover designers, personal assistants, various different courses, pieces of software, services... It can be overwhelming to look out there and see all the various people ready and salivating at the idea of parting prospective authors from their money. And there are a *lot* of sharks. I am going to discuss more about *that* in later chapters, too. Protecting yourself from scammers is an important element to these decisions.

However, zeroing back into the things that you need to spend money on in order to publish a book, here is a list of items that come with price tags in publishing. Remember, I will be talking about how to cut these, but to give you a rough idea of how much that $10k number can be broken down, here's a list of common prices:

Book Costs Explained

- Editing ($800 - $5,000)
- Typesetting ($50 - $500)
- E-book Formatting ($25 - $250-ish)
- Cover Design ($35 - $1,500)
- ISBN ($125/per in the US or $295 for 10)
- Author Website Hosting (variable)
- Distribution (variable)
- Purchasing Author Copies (variable)
- Advertising (Amazon/Facebook etc., variable)
- Marketing (selling at a table for a local convention, printing up cards, etc., variable)

For an updated list based on the time you're reading this, I highly encourage you to check out the Editorial Freelancers Association rate sheet (http://www.the-efa. org). It's updated every few years and has the average pricing for professionals across many genres and types of work listed. The rates sheet is publicly available and is a gold standard.

There are obviously many more things one can spend money on, such as courses on marketing, assets for marketing, and much more, but these are some of the core costs you should expect. If you are going the traditional route, you will likely be responsible for vastly fewer of them, including editing, typesetting, formatting, cover design, ISBN, and distribution. However, you will still need to do things like buy author copies, pay for tables at events you're going to sell at, and so on. Lower costs is not no costs.

The above list is a very, very rough sketch of what some of those things can cost and also is written with fiction in mind. If you are writing a very short chapter book, obviously, editing will cost less. There are many variations on these numbers, and I cannot account for every single possible book in this list. There are also things you may need that are not on this list, such as illustrations or interior design on a book if you have a very design-heavy non-fiction, for example.

My understanding of these prices is based on the time of writing (2023), and on my experience in the publishing industry. It isn't coming out of nowhere or just based on what I see on the internet. I have done every single one of the jobs on this list and have been part of the publishing world since 2008.

My final note on financial considerations is this: *Publishing is one of those businesses where you usually get what you pay for.* I say "usually" because there are scammers who will charge an egregious sum, but typically, they are out there trying to undercut professionals. If you see someone offering to do line edits on a 65k-word book for $100, run. I am not going to denigrate editing colleagues who choose to charge low rates in this industry, but if you've gotten pitches from professionals, going with the cheapest option is unlikely to get you the best results. Cover design is similar a large percentage of the time. However, there are some really solid cover designers out there who are extremely cheap. They do, however, require that you go to them with stock art, and they essentially assemble it for you. In order to make the best use of those types of services, you need to invest the time and expertise into knowing what you need for your genre and in purchasing stock art, so while the design services may be cheap, they're not quite as cheap as they may seem.

On average, a solid photo-manipulated cover made from stock assets will run you somewhere between $150 to $300. The higher rate listed above would be if you hire someone from the high end of the industry to custom design a cover for you that likely includes hand painted work.

Recognizing Market Trends

As with all businesses out there, there are market trends in publishing. These can include tropes that are hot right now, genres that are hot right now, and more. This means you are going to need to keep at least somewhat aware of what books are coming out where and knowing what things are big in your genre right now. You don't need to know the industry as a whole, of course; you can get away with just knowing your piece of it.

Again, this is one of those things you don't need to think about *quite* as hard if you're going traditional, but it is an important consideration because publishers often will be looking for books that are compliant with current trends or at the very least compatible with them. I point you toward the vampire fiction proliferation around the success of *Twilight*. They do, however, also look for things that might interest readers when the current market is saturated.

So how do you identify what's hot right now?

Look at the top sellers in your genre and see what they're doing. Also, look at media in your genre. The media and entertainment ecosystem often works as a whole in many ways despite books and movies and so on being very different beasties when it comes to specifics. See if you can find reading groups that are full of your target audience and ask them for book recommendations. See what people are posting about on GoodReads, TikTok, and other social media platforms. Again, this needs to be focused on your genre. What's big in romance won't really have a lot of crossover with what's big in military sci-fi at any given time.

The point of this is to see what these books have in common with one another and identify broader trends. For example, in paranormal, supernatural fantasy, and urban fantasy, there's a big trend of writing investigators who deal with the magical world. There is also the usual divide of the magical world being hidden from the real one, which is even evident in many of the YA magical academies books that use the real world as part of their storytelling. Other trends may include having more diverse casts of characters, a heightened rate of inclusion for LGBTQIA+ folks, and other elements. Snarky, wisecracking leads are also a genre trend in these spheres (at the time of writing).

All these elements can be used to help your book conform a little more with genre expectations. Or, if you decide to eschew them, you will at least be doing so with full knowledge and understanding of that decision. The key here is to recognize these elements to allow you to make *informed* decisions about your book and the elements you choose to utilize while writing it.

Writing to Market

As I briefly touched on in the last segment, identifying and then putting to use current trends in publishing is extremely important. We call this process "writing to market." There are authors who choose not to write to market and instead focus their time and energy on writing books that they believe will stand the test of time and ignore current trends. That is a fair and reasonable angle. However, if you are looking to make money on your writing in the short term? Writing to market is going to be a significant part of the puzzle.

One important thing I need to address immediately is this: *Writing to market does not mean writing crap at high volume.*

I am not going to suggest you churn out a bunch of low-quality and low-effort books just to chase genre trends. That absolutely is a tactic that some writers use paired with rapid release strategies. Some people write good-quality books quickly and do rapid release that way as well—I'm not knocking them! I view it in the same way I view most products I buy from the dollar store. Are those companies making a profit producing large numbers of low-quality items to people who accept and understand that transaction? Absolutely they are. I point you toward dollar stores, Walmart, Sam's Club, and most bargain and big box stores. The shelves there are littered with exactly those items. There are also people who will purchase nothing but the finest, highest quality, and most expensive items in the market from elite boutiques.

Most of us, if we're honest with ourselves, fall somewhere on that gradient with the majority leaning toward not being above going to the dollar store if we think it has what we need at a price point we are comfortable with.

There are an unfortunate number of people who like to stick their nose in the air at this and imply that authors who write to market are lesser than authors who write for the "sake of the craft." I think that's just a form of elitism those people employ because they're bitter, if I'm honest. It's the same sort of people who talk down about comic book artists or other artists who do commissioned art because it's not "high art" or "challenging the art world." That elitism is nonsense. Most of the people who hold those opinions can't write (or paint or compose or...) their way out of a paper bag. It's very rare that truly preeminent artists of any type will look at others with that sort of sneering self-importance.

I'm a firm believer that the concept of art (and writing is a form thereof) is big enough to encompass the things that both push the boundaries of art and drive the world into new and broader understandings *and* include things that people produce that are closer to what the masses enjoy. Just like I can thoroughly enjoy an artisan loaf of bread and keep sliced white bread in my pantry for sandwiches. There's a market and room for both these things.

Writing to market doesn't mean you have to be the Wonder Bread of books. You can make something that is both good quality and accessible. More to the point, that kind of work is the *one that will be most likely to sell*. If you're reading this because you want to sell books, that should be something you keep in mind. For every lovingly crafted and expensive artisan loaf of bread I buy at a bakery to pair with the perfect soup or to serve with just the right cheese at an event, I devour several cheaper loaves of inexpensive sliced white bread with peanut butter at 2 a.m.

Over time. Not all at once. Please don't picture me as the 2 a.m. peanut butter gremlin just sitting on the floor devouring entire loaves of bread.

I sit at the table, thanks.

Profit is not a dirty word, and if you are entering into book publishing in order to turn one, you need to find the balance between artisan works and things that will provide you more frequent income but may be less high art. There's no wrong answer here, really. You can *also do both*. It's possible to write more artistic works while also developing a library of books that will help you draw income if being a full-time writer is your goal. You can also go through phases in your career over time.

If this sounds like I'm trying to push you to write to market, please understand that my goal here is to lay out in clear language what the options are and strip away some of the stigmas people have about the process. You don't *need* to write to market. It will, however, help you sell books, and that's what you came to me for advice about.

Separating Art from Business

At this stage, when we are looking to sell our book, this is where our mindset must change, which is what this whole chapter has been working toward. The craft of writing is an art form, just like music, painting, dance, or any other. Art has intrinsic value just for existing and making the world more beautiful for it or expressing an emotion the creator has no other way to express. Art is valuable for a whole host of reasons that have nothing to do with money.

Unfortunately, however, we live in a world of money, and choosing to sell that art for money means we have to change our view of our artwork. No longer merely of value for its existence and creative process, it must become a *product*.

Yes, that sounds soulless and awful, and in some ways, it is. I'm not advising you to delete your creativity and artistry, but when we shift our perspective and view this as a business, we absolutely must consider our artwork as a product for sale.

If we are selling our books as a product, that means we need to evaluate them differently. As a product, they must somehow enrich or enhance the life of the person purchasing it. If I buy a candy bar, it's because it will give me some dopamine while I eat it. If I purchase a pretty dress, it's because it will make me happy while I'm wearing it. If I purchase a new chef's knife, it's because it will improve my experience while cooking. A product performs a function, even if that function is only to bring pleasure to the person purchasing it for a short time.

Our *art* has many functions beyond just bringing pleasure to the reader, but our *product* must, at the very least, bring pleasure, amusement, or enrichment somehow. If we are to do that, we need to consider the balance between quality and cost, marketing and staying true to ourselves, and so on. These are all cost-benefit analyses like I mentioned in the earlier section about finances.

For the rest of this book, I will be addressing your manuscript as a product, not purely as a creation of artwork whose value is unquestioned. From here on, we view this through the lens of providing a high-quality *product* to readers and how we can go about creating that and develop the process by which we can bring said *product* to our buyers. We move from the sphere of embracing art as art and into recognizing business as business.

I'm not going to lie to you and pretend that this mindset shift is easy. It's best undertaken after you're done with the manuscript. Evaluating your book as a product while you're writing will hurt your writing process and will stomp on your creativity. I don't advise doing that.

And if all this sounds like an awful lot of misery and work that will destroy your soul to have to consider these elements and do this business? There are two avenues open to you: writing purely for pleasure, and considering traditional publishing. Writing purely for pleasure and enrichment is a worthy pursuit. Not every hobby needs monetization. Not every story on Wattpad people read and enjoy must be sold on Barnes and Noble's shelves. Don't let anybody tell you otherwise. If you read this section and felt your creativity dying, then perhaps publishing as a business isn't meant for you.

Alternatively, you could decide to go into traditional publishing, where the business decisions will be made by people whose minds work in that way and whose hearts beat a little faster when they think of profit and loss statements or other elements of business. Or, at the very least, whose souls don't shrink from the prospect. It's okay if yours does—very rarely does an artist think and view the world like a business-minded person. Often, those pursuits are deeply at odds with one another. You are hardly an outlier for struggling with the idea of trying to be both.

Which leads us directly to our next chapter: How do you choose between methods of publishing?

Summary

Through the course of this chapter, we expanded upon the idea of becoming a businessperson versus just being a private individual. This covered things like how to make certain kinds of decisions, how to analyze things in a way that may be new to you, and learning how to consider your art as a business as well as maintaining that separation between your artist self and your business self.

Key Takeaways

- Making business decisions is a process that can be followed and is not extremely complex but, much like switching from being a writer to being an author, requires us to evaluate things in a new manner.

- Looking at decisions from the perspective of cost-benefit provides us insight into how we can invest in ourselves as a business industry.

- Identifying your audience's expectations and knowing what trends are out there in the world right now can help you position your book effectively in the market.

- It may feel uncomfortable at first to think of your book as a product for sale, but the ability to separate your art from your business strategy is key for success as a published author.

Chapter Three

Paths to Publication

Not counting hybrid presses—which are often vanity presses in disguise and require a great deal of extra scrutiny—there are two main spheres of publishing: traditional publishing and self-publishing. While there are some fuddy-duddies who insist that self-publishing is worthless and traditional is the *only true way*, those people belong back in the 1990s before the rise of self-publishing began.

In the modern era, self-publishing and indie authors are developing a tremendous amount of tools and recognition. The ability to distribute in ways heretofore only accessible by the traditional publishing houses has stripped away one of the major hurdles keeping people from publishing anything and everything they feel like selling to the public—for better or worse.

You will see this reflected in nearly every element of this book, but I want to say firmly and without question before we discuss the paths that *there is no one true way*. There is only the way that works best for you or makes the most sense for your life. Discounting falling prey to predatory practices, the only "wrong" way to publish is the way that doesn't work for you and doesn't allow you to reach your goals.

So with that established, let's talk a little about the two paths in broad terms before we get into the meat and potatoes of the differences between the options you have as an author.

When we look at the publishing sphere as a whole, the primary and most crucial difference between self-publishing and traditional publishing is who absorbs the overhead.

With self-publishing, the person absorbing the overhead is the author. That means you are responsible for funding the production of your book and handling all the elements thereof. It means you are responsible for finding and assembling your team of professionals and then paying them. You also are solely responsible for paying for marketing costs, production costs, and all the other incidentals that come with doing business, like paying for your website hosting. In return, you receive all the earnings.

Alternatively, with traditional publishing, the publisher absorbs the overhead. They hire professionals to handle all aspects of the publishing process, handle the costs associated with advertising, some of the marketing costs, all the costs of production, and all the other elements associated with publishing and running a business. As a result, in order to pay for the costs associated with your book, pay for the costs associated with running a business, and be able to retain profits, the author is paid a relatively small portion of the proceeds in addition to a possible advance. Not all publishers offer advances to all authors in the modern era.

I'll get more specific about royalty rates in the next section, but as with many other things, please be aware that these are the cases in the year 2023. They may be different when you read this book, so please look for updated information if you are reading this book in the future. (And if you are, how *is* the future? Do we have flying cars yet?)

Benefits and Drawbacks of the Paths

Both methods of publishing have pros and cons associated with them. They are neither all good nor all bad. In order to make an effective decision, however, we need to take a look at what those pros and cons are.

As a reminder, I owned a traditional publishing company and worked for another for many years. I am self-publishing my books at this point in my life and work almost exclusively for indie authors. Both sides of the fence are familiar to me, and I am going to try and offer you as unbiased an opinion as I can possibly share.

Doing the Math

Now that we've identified the two main options—again, eschewing hybrid because that is an entire discussion in and of itself that I will put at the end of this chapter—let's look at the benefits and drawbacks of each. As someone who has been on both sides of the publishing line, I don't have a particular horse in this race. Choosing the option that best suits your needs is the goal here, not me preaching the gospel of whatever I prefer.

You also have the option of doing both for different projects. You can self-publish books you know your publisher wouldn't be interested in or pursue a publishing deal while self-publishing other works. Just recognize that, if you're trying to convince a publisher or agent to pick up an already-published work, you're going to have an uphill battle.

While I am going to provide you a convenient table to compare the pros and cons below, please recognize that the table cannot account for everything. Despite indie publishers having a lot of very loud and very angry opinions about traditional publishing and everything it stands for—and a great deal of valid and pointed critique about the representation of those who aren't cishet white people—they still have a role in the world. And it's an important one.

Many authors hit the place where they want to publish a book and see self-publishing as the path of least resistance and view it as a way they can skip the line. While this certainly *can* be true, you run into a problem that has plagued people for a very long time.

The old saying is: fast, good, cheap—you can only pick two. It's been true since time immemorial. Can things be done inexpensively and well? Of course, but it takes a great deal of time. One way or another, equity must be put into the publishing process. Shortcutting that is the way to failure.

What I'm getting at here is that self-publishing at the same quality standards as a traditional publisher to create the best possible product is not cheap in terms of actual money or in terms of equity. Equity here means things that perhaps you do to add value but isn't something where money changes hands, such as learning to design your own book covers through deep study. Will that be technically cheaper than hiring a cover designer? Yes, in terms of dollars in the bank, it will be. But in terms of sweat equity, you're talking the same cost.

If you neglect to put in the time (study) or money (hiring a professional), then you will get fast and cheap, but it will not result in profits.

The reason I bring this up now is because this is the crux of your decision as to which direction you go. If you don't have the money and/or time to effectively self-publish, then traditional is an option that may well have a great deal of interest for you.

Traditional Publishing

Pros	Cons
All proceeds of sales go directly to you	Publishing can be expensive, and you need to foot the entire bill for the overhead
Will retain complete creative control of all decisions	Having complete control may be a challenge if you are not familiar with the industry
Retain complete rights to all of your intellectual property	Creating a publishing team can be challenging to do on your own
Have total control over all business decisions and can shape your business however you like	It can be more challenging to get into certain spaces without a publisher's backing

Self-Publishing

Pros	Cons
Don't need to cover overhead yourself	Receive a smaller paycheck than if self-publishing
Will work with an established team of professionals	Do not retain complete ownership of your intellectual property
Will have marketing and advertising assistance	Will still have to do a lot of the marketing yourself
Don't need to handle all the business decisions on your own	Have little or no decision-making power when it comes to publication

As you can see above, both methods have value for authors. Not having to do all the work yourself or assemble your own team, or pay them, is a significant appeal to folks who just plain don't have the business end of things nailed down. For people who are more comfortable with business or who are willing to become so, self-publishing can certainly net you the highest profits in the shortest amount of time.

On the other hand, traditional publishing—particularly with the Big 5—does have the highest likelihood of making movie deals and can catapult authors to success in ways that self-publishing and even indie publishers cannot. The tradeoff is that you have to get their attention, and there's no sure bet that you'll be one of the lucky few they pick up.

Of course, there's the third route where you shoot for one of the Big 5 for a while, and if they don't bite, you self-publish. That is absolutely a fair option, and one many authors take.

Choosing the Correct Path for You

Up to this point, I've not given any specific advice as to which direction you should take other than a few vague statements about the type of author who might thrive best with which method. In this section, I'm going to dig a little deeper. This segment is also going to contain some pretty harsh realities because I believe in being direct and honest rather than necessarily making everyone feel optimistic about things. I don't want to discourage people from chasing their dreams, but I fully believe there are mistakes that can be made along this path that I would much rather guide you away from. If that means giving somewhat painful advice, then so be it.

With that in mind, let's look at questions you can ask yourself to identify which path is going to be the best one for you and your career.

Can you absorb the overhead?

As stated in the "Financial Considerations" segment in Chapter 3, *publishing is expensive*. I don't mean to sound like a gatekeeper, but starting a business for yourself is not cheap. Furthermore, it's a risk. You could invest an awful lot of money into a book that flops because of any number of reasons. If your book flops, will it devastate you in a way you cannot recover from? If the answer to that is *yes*, then chances are you will want to consider traditional publishing.

Are you able to put in the work?

As much as we might have rose-colored glasses about our own capabilities at times (past me is always more optimistic about what present me can do than present me is), we need to evaluate this with the cold ruthlessness of a computer. No matter which path you take, there will be work inherent in it, but of the two, self-publishing requires a whole lot more direct and immediate work in order to be successful.

As much as I might want to phrase this question in a more delicate manner, I went with "able" because we need to be honest and realistic. If you don't have 5-20 hours a week to put into nothing but your publishing work—and the number will fluctuate depending on what phase you're in—then you're not *able* to do the work. While you're preparing for release, you might spend several months putting 20+ hours a week into your book launch.

If you cannot make that kind of commitment, you might want to factor that into your plans. While traditional publishing will still demand time every week for marketing activities, you won't have quite as much to do prior to launch—unless you are lucky enough to get sent on book tours all over the world like the big names do. You will, however, need to dedicate time to doing things like going to local events, doing signings, and planning for those things. Whether self-published or traditional, you *must* dedicate time on a regular basis to your work if you are going to be successful.

This does not omit real life, however. You will have seasons of life where you are going to be more focused on other things due to necessity or interest (things like sickness, children, partners needing care, parents needing care, etc.). That's a given, and it's to be expected in the context of a longer term career. Life happens. I don't want you to say, "But E. said to never take breaks!" That's not what I'm getting at here. This is intended to be broad-scope advice. If you need time off, take it. And if you needed permission to take that time off, this is that permission. Right here. Take time off.

Is this a career or a hobby?

There is nothing wrong if your book publishing is a hobby. If you view it as a thing you want to dabble in to maybe earn some income doing something you find personally rewarding, that is a perfectly valid reality for you. I have many hobbies myself. Some are more expensive than others (I'm squinting at you, Society for Creative Anachronism). I draw and sell fantasy maps as *mostly* a hobby at the moment. I find it rewarding, and every so often, someone throws money at me. It's a good arrangement.

However, if you want your writing to become your *career*, you need to treat it with the gravitas that is due. If writing is going to be your career, it means accepting a lot of rejection, making expensive mistakes here and there, and continuing to push even when it stops being fun. Because *there are going to be times where this whole writing-and-publishing thing is not fun.*

With a hobby, you should feel no sense of failure or have a major financial impact if you set it aside. You'll have feelings about not doing it anymore, certainly, but it won't cause a hole in your foundational life goals, generally speaking. The same is not true for a career.

Are you able and willing to learn the ins and outs of the business?

I say "able" more as a function of time than intellectual capacity. That said, business terrifies some people, and there are individuals in the world who just cannot think in terms of it. There's nothing wrong with that if that's who you are. Truly. If that *is* who you are, however, you are likely better off going the traditional publishing route unless you plan to hire someone to handle those things for you. Also, recognize that you will still be expected to handle business stuff if you go traditional. I remind you that marketing is an ever-present reality.

Self-publishing is, by its nature, a business. It comprises of far more than writing a book and uploading it to Amazon, after all, and requires a lot of decisions, such as the ones discussed in this book thus far. While going the traditional publishing route also requires you to make decisions, they are less about numbers and more about finding the right publisher and agent for you as well as marketing choices.

While I know I keep hammering home the fact that self-publishing is not for everyone, I believe in making sure people enter into these situations with awareness and intent. I don't want anybody stumbling around in the dark, groping for a light switch when it comes to these choices.

There is also a fad surrounding self-publishing of people saying it's "easy." This is because querying is *hard*. Finding the right agent or publisher is not an easy thing to do, and it comes with a lot of rejection because the business is both highly competitive and full of people who have specific desires. If you don't hit those notes, you won't find someone. The good news is that, while there's a lot of start and stop involved, the publishing world is big enough that there are a number of truly wonderful options who may fit your book.

Can you handle rejection and criticism?

No matter which route you take, you will face both rejection and criticism. Readers will leave bad reviews. Literary critics might decline to review your book or give you a bad review. Agents and publishers can and will reject you. All these things are realities. There is no getting around them.

You might think that you will be *the one* who doesn't experience those things, and I wish you luck if you feel that way. However, you need to be prepared to take hard knocks. To take rejection letters and bad reviews. To take critiques from people at all levels of the game, including other authors. If you cannot field those experiences, publishing may not be for you at all, let alone determining which direction you go.

That isn't to say you will necessarily be treated abysmally by everybody. You won't. But the road to publishing is paved with rejection letters, and that is a reality of the industry. It's hard and painful. However, I personally think it's worth it.

Even after you've published the book, you will get bad reviews or have people decline to take you as a speaker, decline to review your book, decline to have you at an event, and so on. You are going to be facing people saying harsh things about your book and potentially about you as a person. Being a public figure is not for the faint of heart. If you respond to this kind of criticism and experience with growling, defensiveness, and reactivity, you will end up setting your career on fire.

There are a number of big names who have done this, and I am not going to name and shame them here, but if you look, you'll find them. Handling these feelings of rejection and being treated in ways you cannot control is *hard*. I've had people come at me a few times, and it hurts every time. When it happens, I retreat into my circle of real-world friends and hide there for a bit.

When this happens to you—when, not if—you should consider how you will handle that kind of thing and go into this expecting it. Don't be terrified because it's one of those things that happens to everyone eventually. Not everyone will like your book. Not everyone will like *you*. That's okay. Just be prepared for it.

Busting Publishing Myths

Some of these are going to be things I've covered elsewhere, but I want to crystalize a few specific points that need to be addressed before we can keep going. Writers' groups are brimming with myths of various kinds, and it drives me up a wall. Not because I want to ruin people's day but because these myths set authors up for failure and misery. They also give people unrealistic expectations of what certain things entail because, frankly, they're wishful thinking.

Myth #1: If you write it, they will come.

This is one of the big ones that most writers walk into the industry believing. They think that if they can just write the book, people will find and buy it. While it's true you will maybe get some readers that way, it's not the road to success. Writing the book is just the first step on the journey, and frankly, it's the easy part.

Just writing the book isn't enough. You need to write it, polish it, make sure you categorize it properly, and then market the hell out of it. You absolutely can write something off the beaten path and find an audience, but you are going to have to *find the audience*. That means connecting with people where they are and knowing where to find them. That takes time, research, and dedication. Learning who your audience is, which I cover in detail in

Chapter 12, is vital to all authors, but it's even more important and complex for those of us writing works that aren't easy to position in the market.

Myth #2: Editors are the antagonists of the writing world.

I've run into this one a lot. People like to cast us as bogeymen out there looking to tear apart and destroy your books. I even had a heckler at a talk I was at threaten me. He asked why I wasn't afraid of the writers in the room because they could tear me apart.

His attempt to intimidate came from the idea that there's an adversarial relationship between editors and authors. There isn't. Nor should there be! Editors, as a whole, are just bespectacled nerds whose whole lives are found in the pages of books. We are more likely to be owlish weirdos who text each other gifs about commas at 3 a.m. No joke. We do that. (Shout out to my 3 a.m. editing meme friends. You know who you are.)

Our goals are to help your books be the best they can possibly be and help you find ways to sell them and be successful. We aren't out here like Snidely Whiplash curling our mustaches at the idea of new authors. As a rule, we are more Abby Scuito from *NCIS* than J. Jonah Jameson. Though I don't think any of us would turn down photos of Spider-Man, particularly Tom Holland. He's precious.

Myth #3: Being traditionally published means you don't have to market.

This is one of the huge bugbears. It is categorically untrue. While a large publisher will have a marketing department, and you will have help with this process from them, you aren't going to be able to do nothing but write and have your books sell well. I had a conversation with Raymond E. Feist, author of *The Riftwar Cycle*, about this fact. He was dragging books around in a wagon to sell them to bookstores before I was even born.

While being traditionally published means you don't have to market alone, and the publisher will handle *advertising*, it doesn't mean you can just write manuscripts, send them in, and then stay in your writing cave forever doing nothing else. You will have to manage your social media, make public appearances, and put work into promoting your book. The work isn't over once the contract is signed.

Myth #4: Traditional publishing is dead.

This one is really popular in some places, and it's just not true. It *is* true that traditional publishing is changing and looks different than it once did. It's true that traditional publishing is not the only answer these days. However, it's absolutely not true that traditional publishing is dying or going away.

With this myth often comes the notion that traditional publishing is somehow bad and that it's a dinosaur. These things are also untrue. Does traditional publishing have gatekeepers who decline or accept manuscripts? Yes. Do traditional publishers under-represent disenfranchised communities? Historically, this is absolutely true. That is changing with time and the rise of indie presses. Is traditional publishing behind the times? It can be in certain areas.

With all those things said, none of them mean it is non-viable or "dying." It is changing. It is different. It requires you to leap some hurdles. It certainly might not pay as well as you might want it to. However, for some people, having another entity handle the overhead is their only way to publish and have even a ghost of a chance at success. There is *nothing* wrong with going the traditional route, just as there is nothing wrong with self-publishing.

Myth #5: Everyone can, and should, self-publish.

Kind of as a counterpart to the last one, some people in the writing world have this idea in their minds that self-publishing is the only way for everybody and that anyone can do it. Both of these things are patently untrue. As I, hopefully, have been explaining through the course of this book, there are multiple routes to success, and the only wrong one is the one that doesn't work for you.

There's also the hard reality that self-publishing effectively costs money—like any business does. It's not free or even cheap, if I'm honest. Whether you pay in money or you pay in time, you still pay. That's the stark reality of the thing. You can minimize costs to some extent, but "minimize" doesn't mean "erase."

Because of this, not everyone can or should self-publish. Trying to suggest to writers that it's the one true way without talking about the financial impact does them a disservice because they then start realizing how expensive it is and become discouraged, publish without adequate work done, or put a lot of money into publishing, only to realize they have no idea how to market, and they are now stuck with a multi-thousand-dollar investment that isn't selling.

Myth #6: All gatekeeping is bad.

The term "gatekeeping" has multiple definitions these days, which muddies the waters during discussion. There is gatekeeping in the sense of what acquisitions editors do, and then there's gatekeeping in the sense of the Urban Dictionary definition, which reads, "When someone takes it upon themselves to decide who does or does not have access or rights to a community or identity."

Obviously, if someone is trying to keep people out of a community or identity—such as saying someone cannot be a fan of a band without being able to cite their entire discography from memory—that is a negative thing. However, there is a significant difference between the person demanding you justify your Metallica T-shirt and someone saying your book is not ready to be published.

The reality is that not every book *should* be published for public consumption. If that sounds harsh, take a breath and keep reading. I'm not suggesting that your book is garbage if it's rejected, but certain works should not see the light of day.

I used to be in acquisitions for publishing companies. I've seen things across my desk that should never be sold or would require such extensive rewrites as to be different books. I'm not talking things based on taste, either. One guy rewrote *The Old Man and the Sea* in "haiku." It wasn't even haiku. The manuscript was truly abysmal, to say nothing of infringing on a very much still-existing United States copyright, and the author grew irate when I rejected it. He called me a "tool of the publishing elite."

If anything at all were to be in print for anybody to buy with no filter whatsoever, there are a lot of truly horrible things that the public would be subjected to. I don't mean niche stuff or things like Chuck Tingle, who is amazing. I mean deeply depraved, horrifying things, like Nazi apologist things. While some publishers will pick that up, they're the minority since they know it won't sell well and will absolutely wreck their credibility. In the days before indie publishing's rise, it was nearly impossible to get something like that out there.

You also have issues with AI-generated works getting poured into Amazon by the bucketload and drowning out authors who actually *wrote their book*. With a lack of gatekeepers standing at the ready, there's nothing to stop that from reaching the general public and forcing consumers to wade through an ocean of hot garbage.

Currently, anybody can upload anything to Amazon that meets their rather loose standards. Granted, it'll probably get buried by the algorithm, and nobody will really see it, but it is still *there*.

Gatekeepers, like acquisitions editors, are only a bad thing if they're being jerks. Those who reject manuscripts from people of color as a categorical thing, or those who refuse LGBTQIA+ books for print and so on? Those are a problem. But protecting the general public from the ravings of your racist uncle about how the Nazis got it right? That's a significant portion of what we do. No joke.

Myth #7: You need to choose one type of publishing and do that forever.

It might feel like you have to choose "A" or "B" sometimes, but the reality is you are not tied to exclusivity.

If you go traditional, you will need to read and study your contract to know what the boundaries are, but there are many authors who do a mix of both very successfully. You can also start in traditional and eventually choose to self-publish (e.g. Brandon Sanderson). Or you can self-publish, decide it's not for you, and shift gears to looking for an agent for your next book.

There is absolutely no shame in doing both, bouncing between the two, or discovering the one you initially chose doesn't work out the way you wish it did and deciding to try the other. You have that right, and nobody is going to stop you from doing that.

Summary

There are many ways you can go from manuscript to published book, and finding the one that best fits you is going to be a function of evaluating what you want from the experience along with what fits your needs. Spending some time evaluating your personal goals will help you choose the direction you want to go.

Key Takeaways

- The only wrong way to go is the one that does not work for you. Don't let anybody try and tell you there is one correct way; that is just not the truth.

- Publishing requires work, no matter which of the various options you land on. There is no "set it and forget it" option if you want to be a successful author.

- Rejection is, unfortunately, part and parcel to making a living as a creative. You cannot avoid some degree of it, and there is no getting around it. Making your peace with that fact can be challenging, but it will be necessary. Also, know that a lot of the rejection you will face is not personal. Your work can be groundbreaking and still not be liked by everyone.

- Regardless of which direction you choose, you will need to educate yourself on the industry and learn as much as you can about it. The more knowledge you have, the better a choice you can make.

- Sometimes the advice in writing groups can be unintentionally misleading. It's not that they're trying to be dishonest, but many of the people giving that advice genuinely don't know what they're doing. Evaluate advice given to you carefully and always look for multiple perspectives.

Chapter Four
Traditional publishing

If, after all your considerations, you choose the path of traditional publishing, there are a lot of moving pieces to it. Just like with self-publishing, there are choices to be made and things to be evaluated. If you aren't choosing traditional publishing, or have no interest in how it will work, you can skip this chapter, and I won't take it personally. Or I'll try not to. I'll just wallow here in my ice cream and sniffle pitifully in your mind's eye. It's okay. No, really.

Joking aside, traditional publishing has a few things you need to decide on, which we're going to discuss in this chapter. There are also pitfalls inherent to it that you need to be aware of and go into with preparation to defend against. As much as I would like to say traditional publishing doesn't have sharks in it, it does. Just like self-publishing, there are predators who lurk in the water, and if you aren't aware of them, you might well get bitten.

Traditional publishing is, as I have said repeatedly, a viable path ideal for people who don't have the money to self-publish and/or those who don't have the confidence or ability to handle all the business elements themselves. If you *do* have the ability or desire to do that, then you'll probably succeed in self-publishing. However, some people don't have the time, energy, money, or desire to handle all those parts. I see you. Those desires are fair and reasonable.

Reflecting back on my myths at the end of the last chapter, choosing traditional publishing doesn't mean you're a failure or that you can't hack it. It just means that your cost-benefit analysis skewed in the direction of having another entity handle the sticky parts. It's like deciding to purchase something rather than make it. Many of us look at crafty things and think, "I don't need to buy that; I could make it." That may be true, but for a large percentage of us, if we're honest with ourselves, we'd rather buy sliced bread than bake bread every day.

This is exactly the same.

There *are* people for whom baking bread every day is their ritual. They find deep fulfillment in it and pay lower grocery bills. There are some people for whom that is a possible and reasonable thing to do because their lives are structured to allow it. Then there are people who absolutely know how to bake bread, enjoy baking bread here and there, but usually buy it because we don't have time or energy to bake as often as we might like.

Choosing Who to Submit Your Manuscript To

Choosing your publisher is going to start with a few questions, just like a lot of these are. The first amongst them is deciding what your goals are. If you want to be the next Stephen King, and you want to make writing the thing you live and breathe—and self-publishing is not a thing you want to do—then you might be best off approaching one of the Big Five (Penguin/Random House, Hachette Book Group, Harper Collins, Simon and Schuster, Macmillan) or their many imprints.

The Big Five are, to be frank, the dream of many of us. It's the "author life" we dream about and see on television (*Murder, She Wrote* and *Castle*, for example). They're the publisher's publishers. For better or for worse, they have been rightfully critiqued many times in many ways. However, if you want your book on shelves in every bookstore, eventually do book tours, or get a movie deal, this is probably going to be the direction you want to look.

If your plan is more modest than that, you might start looking at the big publishers who aren't the Big Five or even indie presses. Often, people start by approaching major publishers and agents first, then decide to approach smaller players if they are struggling to get accepted. That's a fair game plan, too.

With publishers, you'll want to make a few notes once you've decided on the scale of the thing. You'll want to consider whether or not that publisher works in your genre, what their reputation is if they have one, and if you feel like you'd mesh with their vibe. You also want to find out if they accept simultaneous submissions, but we'll talk a little more about that in the query section.

Do You Need an Agent?

If you want to go with a large publisher, your first stop will probably be to find an agent. Agents who work in your genre can be found in many places, and locating legitimate literary agents can be a difficult but worthwhile procedure. I personally suggest starting with industry publications and Duotrope. You can find a lot of people in those places and identify people who have worked with authors publishing comparable pieces to yours.

Working with an agent can be tough, and they do take a cut of your profits. They also, however, act as a shepherd through the publication process. No small part of their job is to make sure you don't get burned, so they are absolutely a worthwhile thing to have. Just make sure you consider them carefully.

Another thing about agents is that they help with the submissions process. Their job is to go between the author and the publisher, so rather than you agonizing over writing the perfect query letter yourself, having an agent can help smooth over the submissions process. They often make recommendations to ensure your book is as print worthy as possible. Agents also help with contracts, and their entire job is to represent their author and get the best they can for said author, so they're worth the cut of your finances if they're good.

On the downside, there are risks associated with working with an agent. Just like with publishers, there are people of questionable moral fiber who set up a shingle and claim to be agents. That, and you are going to be paying your agent *forever*. They take a cut of book sales, film sales, and so on. This person will ostensibly receive money from your cut of your earnings for a long time. Authors already don't live high on the hog, so this consideration may be worth giving a hard think. As always, it comes down to a cost-benefit.

Many publishers also do not accept submissions except from authors represented by agents, so if your goals include the big companies, you may need to bite the bullet and solicit one. Either that, or aim your sights on an imprint or publisher who doesn't require authors be represented by agents.

Query Letters and How to Write Them

Requests for help putting together a query is one of the things I see over and over again in writing spheres. It's a foreign kind of writing that we fiction writers are often averse to. It also doesn't help that many of us think too far outside the box to craft them in ways that over-stressed acquisitions people want. In this segment, I'm going to cover some of the principles of writing a good query that you can take forward, but I want to start by saying the obvious that so many people neglect: *Read the query guidelines and follow them.*

Query Basics

Personally, I think I'd call querying the "special hell" that Shepherd Book talks about in *Firefly*. It's stressful, painful, and takes forever. You also need to be aware that if you are querying, unless you're represented by an agent, there's a good chance you are going to be sending out that query to *one publisher at a time*. This is because simultaneous submissions are considered a waste of time for a large number of publishers. I'll get into that more when we talk about what they contain.

In essence, query letters are your handshake to the publishing company. You introduce yourself, your book, and give them a taste of what to expect from you. Companies all have their individual guidelines, but I feel safe in telling you to expect and prepare these few things for a query letter:

- A short introduction to who you are
- The word count of your book
- The genre of your book
- A very short elevator pitch regarding what your book is about
- The first 1-3 chapters (this will vary depending on the publisher; some may have a word count specified)
- A synopsis of your book

As I said above, publishers have their own guidelines about the details of those things, but those are what you can expect to see on most publisher's list of things they want. Some publishers want fewer things than that. Some may want more.

Beyond the specifics of what you include, you will want your query letter to be three things: brief, polished, personal. In order to explain why, I'm going to give you a bit of a peek behind the curtain into what it's like to be an acquisitions editor.

The reality of the job is receiving dozens or hundreds of manuscripts a day a lot of the time. Whether you have a team of acquisitions editors, as larger publishers do, or just one, their job is to evaluate as quickly as possible whether or not the book is correct for their publishing house and for this place in the season.

As such, you want to make the acquisitions editor's job as easy as possible. Keeping your email succinct and to the point helps a lot. Also, avoid fancy formatting, colors, or images. Generally speaking, those just slow the process down, and most of the time, the people who do that are trying to get attention in the wrong way.

Why the Guidelines Matter

When I was doing the job, the things that attracted me to a query were whether or not the letter was written well, showed a little of the author's spirit and voice, and whether or not they followed the guidelines. Following the guidelines was an instant mark in their favor given how frequent it is that authors think the query guidelines aren't firm and are mere suggestions. These are not the pirate code. Trust me.

Following the query guidelines, and doing so with panache, is going to get you more attention than flouting them.

With the understanding that the person who is reading your email is likely drowning in book pitches, you can see why keeping things tight, clear, and providing a little personal touch will make a difference. Personal touch mostly shows though in how you approach the letter. Staying business formal isn't a bad thing, but showing a little of your humanity helps, particularly if you can make someone smile. Also, if possible, using the query editor's name shows you actually looked around the website and aren't just spamming queries helter skelter.

An important thing to note here: If the publisher says they don't accept simultaneous submissions or that they expect you to label them, *they mean it*. Be honest and upfront about that. Don't just leave it out and hope. You'd be amazed how often acquisitions editors talk in various places online, and if you are breaking the rules and ignoring that, they will probably figure it out eventually. And they will be very annoyed.

While you may think that you sending the first few pages of the manuscript will "only take them ten minutes to read," you're both underestimating the work that goes into an evaluation and overestimating their time. Evaluating a query means running through a mental bullet list. It can be very easy to chuck someone into the "form rejection letter" bin if they don't comply with guidelines because that takes longer to evaluate. If you get to the point where they are actually going to read the synopsis and sample pages you send, recognize that kind of consideration is not easy. It might be fast, and it may be relatively simple, but it's not easy.

The reason publishers ask you not to do simultaneous submissions, where you send out queries to everybody, is often that it is a waste of their time. If you're going to be getting messages back from fifteen different publishers, they're going to have to wait for your reply or become abruptly aware that you have wasted their time.

I know that sounds harsh, but please remember that these people drink from the firehose of bad writing all day, every day. I received queries that still provoke rants if I talk about them (e.g., haiku man). There's a hilarious book out there titled *Why Editors Drink*, and I related completely to every piece of it. Standing out amongst that morass requires professionalism, polish, focus, and being a good fit for that publisher in particular.

The last thing I'm going to say here is, if you do receive a rejection, please don't reply to it. You can, if you must, send a polite, "Thank you for your time!" email in a pleasant tone, but leave it there. The number of angry, nasty, hate-filled messages I got while I was in acquisitions was immense. Yes, we laugh about them behind the scenes. Yes, we talk about it when you act that way—and yes, we tell other editors to not accept submissions from you.

A prospective author who melts down and sends a rage-filled screed to a rejecting editor is, in our industry, a bullet dodged. We also tell other people about it, so you might end up very quietly blacklisted if you behave like a jerk.

What Acquisitions Editors Look For

So, now that I've told you a little bit about what it's like to be one of these people, let's get into what we look for. The things that really catch our eye. My goal is to be as transparent about this as possible because there's no need for smoke and mirrors here.

I could tell in the first couple paragraphs, most of the time, if the manuscript is ready for publishing or something my company was going to invest in. Yes, I hear you crying that it isn't enough, and your book deserves a fairer shake than that! The reality is that many of us can identify in a matter of sentences if a book is going to be a nightmare to work on. That said, if we ask for the whole manuscript, we really do read it. So, what are acquisitions editors really looking for in a query?

Before you panic, the answer here isn't "perfection."

In the Query:

- Adherence to guidelines
- Professionalism and tone
- Good punctuation and grammar
- Clarity of purpose and goals
- A genre that meshes with the publisher's
- A word count that falls within our parameters
- Understanding of their target market

In the Excerpt:

- Polished prose (minimal typos and grammar errors)
- Interesting characters
- Avoidance of literary quagmires (purple prose, boring openings, etc.)
- Voice markers indicating solid voice and clarity
- Obvious understanding of the craft

In the Synopsis:

- Clear presentation of the ideas of the story
- Understanding of story arcs and construction
- Conformation with genre expectations (within reason)
- An understanding of what a synopsis is

The goal of a query letter is to display to the person reading it that you understand your genre, understand your audience, are a capable writer, and aren't going to be a nightmare to work with. Editors over the years develop a sixth (or seventh or eighth…) sense when it comes to red flags with clients. We look for them constantly and are aware when they pop up. If you fear being flagged, however, there's a good chance you won't be.

Red flags can include things like not following guidelines—which shows poor attention to detail or a lack of respect—a tone that suggests the author is self-important (it happens a lot), people who immediately expect you to make exceptions for their *literary genius*, and so on. These flags indicate authors who are going to be profoundly difficult to work with. And of course, if someone is extremely difficult to work with, we are likely to pass on them unless they possess some kind of unique literary genius. Very, very few people ever rise to that level. Those who do are usually gems to work with anyway. (Garth Nix is tremendously nice and very warm and kind, for example.)

Writing a Synopsis

The part of querying the majority of writers dread most is, in fact, the synopsis. While I know this sounds like the worst thing ever, keep in mind that you want to provide the agent/editor with a snapshot of the arc of your story. You don't need to tell us every little thing or write out the whole book.

The goal with the synopsis is to show the core of the story and to give a snapshot of the main character(s). You'll want to shoot for no more than 1,000 words maximum—500 if you can swing it—and keep it tight and clean. If you absolutely cannot keep it that short, do your best to stay as short and succinct as possible. Remember, these are busy people, and your book is one of dozens they might be reviewing that day.

How do we do this? There are many formulas, and there's no "one correct way." However, in the interest of giving you some guidelines, consider doing things in this order:

- Introduce main character (1-3 sentences) and their motivations (1-2 sentences)
- Introduce primary conflict (1-3 sentences)
- Midpoint (1-3 sentence)
- Dark night of the soul (1-3 sentences)
- Finale (1-3 sentences)
- Conclusion (1-3 sentences)

If this looks an awful lot like the Beat Sheet, that's because I am recommending you identify key moments in the sheet to display the arc of your story. If you have no idea what the Beat Sheet is, I suggest you either read the first book in this two-book set where I explain it, or pick up a copy of *Save the Cat* by Blake Snyder since he's the one who came up with it.

The goal here is to keep the detail level low, hit the major points of the story, and get out. You don't need to explain much and should not mention all the characters. Keep your focus on key characters (protagonist, antagonist, important secondary) and don't wander into the weeds. In addition, don't hold back on spoilers. The editor is not your target audience, and they expect spoilers with these, so don't keep back the juicy bits. You want to capture their interest.

Part of capturing their interest will also mean doing so in a way that tells a story. For example, let's give this a go on *Star Wars, Episode IV*:

Luke Skywalker lives on a backwater planet and works for his uncle on their moisture farm. He dreams of becoming a pilot someday and maybe joining the military, but his uncle doesn't believe he's ready and is trying to convince him to stay.

When his family comes into possession of a droid on a mission, Luke meets up with a hermit who lives nearby: Ben Kenobi. When he meets Ben, the droid plays a frantic message from Princess Leia, leader of the rebellion fighting against the Galactic Empire. Ben, known also as Obi-Wan Kenobi, asks Luke to join him in his quest to help Princess Leia. Luke turns him down. But when he returns home and discovers the Empire has killed his aunt and uncle and razed his home, he has no choice but to go with Obi-Wan to try and escape the same fate.

Luke and Obi-Wan go to the nearby spaceport of Mos Isley to try and secure a ride off the planet and meet Han Solo, a smuggler of questionable morality, who agrees to get them off-world on his ship, The Millennium Falcon.

Elsewhere, on a spaceship known as the Death Star, the Empire attempts to force Princess Leia to give up the rebels by threatening to destroy her home planet of Alderaan. Unable to withstand their interrogation, she gives up the location of the rebel base. Then, to demonstrate the power of the Death Star, the Empire destroys Alderaan anyway.

On the Millennium Falcon, Obi-Wan Kenobi senses the destruction of the planet. Knowing that the Empire is hot on their heels, he begins training Luke in the ways of combat in "the Force" to help prepare him for the fight ahead. When the Millennium Falcon arrives to where Alderaan should be, the Death Star captures the ship.

The main characters avoid being caught by hiding in a smuggling compartment, and Luke and Han Solo leave the ship to try and rescue Princess Leia while Obi-Wan provides a distraction by confronting Darth Vader, the man in charge of the Death Star. He challenges Darth Vader to a duel and dies in the process.

Luke and Han successfully rescue Princess Leia and barely manage to escape the Death Star, leaving on the Millennium Falcon to try and beat the Death Star to the location of the rebel base. They arrive, and the rebels formulate a plan to fight the Death Star. It is revealed that there is a small exhaust port they can attack in order to take it down.

The climax of the story is the rebels destroying the Death Star together, preserving the rebels and striking a terrible blow to the Galactic Empire.

At 447 words, that synopsis is tight and tells the rough parts of the story that give you a snapshot of what it's about. I *only* name the characters who have a large impact on the story and don't bother giving any backstory. I also tried to make it at least somewhat interesting to read rather than an empty recitation of the events of the story because going with a "this happens, then this happens, then this happens" approach may be accurate, but it's *boring*. If you want to stand out, your synopsis should be at least as palatable as you can get it.

As I said at the outset, however, perfection isn't your goal. You want *good*.

Talking About Yourself

One of the things about querying that trips people up is talking about themselves. Sure, you could give a CV, which is useful if you're writing non-fiction related to an area of expertise, but what you want to consider is flavor and voice. If you're stuck, take a look at the bios of writers who work in your genre and copy the format.

Mine, for example, was created to follow the flow of Jim Butcher's. It's not exact, but I looked at his biography and the tone he used and followed in his footsteps. You don't need to write anything long, just a few lines about who you are, what genre(s) you write, what experience you have, and a nod to any interesting hobbies. For example, when I tell people I do historical reenactment and sword fighting, people tend to get very interested. If you don't have any hobbies that you consider interesting—though they all are, I promise—you can mention pets, your family, or interests. Remember, you're looking for short and sweet here.

Handling Rejection

Rejection sucks. I'm not going to sugar coat that. The experience of being told, "Thanks, no thanks," or worse, hearing absolutely nothing is grinding. As a neurodivergent person with RSD (rejection-sensitive dysphoria), I understand this on a bone-deep level.

Hearing anything that I perceive as rejection feels like dying. It's horrible, and it leads me to question every element of my existence and value.

So how the hell am *I* a writer? The first step is to recognize that rejection *will* happen. It's not an "if," it's a "when." The second step is to understand that rejection from publishers and agents and even reviewers isn't about me. Having a manuscript rejected may have absolutely nothing to do with my ability to write whatsoever. That publisher might just not have a slot on their publication schedule for a book of that genre/type, maybe they don't feel like they click with me as a person, or about a million other possible reasons that have nothing to do with me.

That doesn't make it hurt less, but it does help in the self-worth department. Understanding that books are regularly rejected for a million and one reasons that have nothing at all to do with whether the author is any good helps. Because it's not always about *you*. I've rejected books that I firmly and with my whole heart believe should be published, but not by me.

For example, many years ago, I turned down a manuscript written by a woman living under Daesh (a more acceptable term for ISIS/ISIL) rule. She was still living there and wanted someone in the West to tell her story. The tiny publisher I was at could not have done so adequately, and furthermore, we would be wholly unequipped if Daesh came after us. When I sent her the rejection, I recommended some people she could contact with her story who would be better able to help. It wasn't that I didn't believe in the story or her, but I just *couldn't*.

There are also plenty of times where I've seen a decent-quality book come across my desk that just wasn't a book I would work well on. When I was an acquisitions editor, it was either me or my editing partner doing the editing in addition to acquisitions. In those situations, I made sure to tell the author that in the rejection, but not every editor has the time or bandwidth to do that. Also, some companies may have a policy against personalizing the rejection letter for all I know.

When I receive a rejection, my reaction is to take a deep breath, close the message, and go do something else for a while. Some people might have a glass of wine, a square of chocolate, or go outside and scream at the sky. All these are reasonable responses. There's no wrong way to feel about rejection in this case. The only wrong way to handle it is to write a nasty email back to the person who sent the rejection detailing how they're wrong, you're right, and how dare they question your genius.

Take a deep breath, take some time to sulk, and keep moving forward.

Identifying Scams and Vanity Presses

The last piece we're going to cover in this segment is handling sharks. The first thing I want to put out on the table is that, if anyone approaches *you* to publish your book, they are one of two things: inexperienced or predatory. Inexperienced editors might approach authors to ask to publish their books. I did that early on in my career a few times, and I know now that it wasn't the way things work. However, I was acting in good faith, and nobody told me not to. Quite the opposite, actually. (I was the receiver of awful advice on that score.)

Predators, however, will approach you and offer things like huge audiences, massive returns, and NYT Bestseller status for the low, low cost of your soul. And probably a lot of money. That's your first red flag. Anyone advertising themselves as a "traditional publisher" or "literary agent" and then asking you to pay them for anything up front is a scam artist. Traditional publishers make their money on book sales, not on authors' pockets. Literary agents make money from royalties, not upfront fees.

There is an exception to this in that hybrid publishers are a legitimate thing, and those who do that often advertise that up front. Hybrid publishers operate by splitting the overhead of publishing the novel in exchange for much more generous royalty rates. Currently, the list of legitimate hybrid publishers is pretty tiny, but it includes Forbes Books, Greenleaf Book Group, Mascot Books, and

Scribe Publishing. However, approach with extreme caution.

There are also self-publishing services companies (like mine, Insomnia Self-Publishing Services) that sell services but take no royalties and don't take intellectual property rights. Those are not to be lumped in with vanity presses or scams unless they're behaving in a predatory manner. Usually, those companies don't call themselves publishers, either.

An excellent resource in navigating these waters is the blog *Writers Beware*. They identify predatory companies, provide resources for identifying people and entities looking to do you harm, and stay up to date on the newest scams on the marketplace. If you are looking to see if a company is legitimate or not, *Writers Beware* should be one of your first stops.

While I am not a lawyer, and nor do I play one on television, you should read any contract provided carefully and ask questions. If it seems "too good to be true," there's a good chance it is, and you'll want to read the entire thing, fine print and all. Don't sign anything with anybody until you've had a chance to review the terms and ensure that you are not being taken for a ride.

When in doubt, contact a lawyer. Any legitimate company will have no issues having a discussion with an attorney if you need to, and they should not discourage you from showing the contract to a legal professional. Make sure you consult a lawyer who is versed in this sphere, however. I've had to field communications from business lawyers who didn't understand publishing as an industry and tried to force things into the contract that wouldn't work in our field. That isn't to say they were acting in bad faith, but it's always best to consult an expert in the field of law you need help in.

The key here is to always do serious and in-depth analysis of anywhere you plan to work with. Vet people, ask questions, ask for testimonials, look for people who have worked with them, and do an internet search with the name of the place you're considering working with and the word "scam" with it.

There's no 100% guarantee in any of this, but doing your due diligence can help cut down the chances of you getting snapped up by con artists by a significant margin.

Summary

Traditional publishing has a number of challenges associated with it, but every path to publishing does. If you keep your eyes open and know what you're looking for, you can avoid many of the pitfalls. These challenges and pitfalls are not insurmountable by any stretch, but they do require being cautious. Utilizing traditional publishing can also make it possible for many authors to get their works to readers without going into debt.

Key Takeaways

- Traditional publishing can remove the cost barriers authors often face with publishing their books. This comes with some sacrifices, but it can be a way for authors who otherwise could not publish to do so.

- While the traditional publishing industry has its problems, there are very real benefits to be found in it for some authors.

- Learning what publishers are looking for and how to approach them will gain you a lot of ground when it comes to the prospect of being picked up by one.

- Vanity presses and scams abound, so do your research and vet the publisher you are going to work with—particularly if they are a hybrid publisher. Anybody promising you the moon is likely a scammer. Also, if they reach out to you first, they are either inexperienced or a scam.

Chapter Five

Publishing in a Nutshell

Okay, now that we've covered traditional publishing, you might be wondering why you should continue on in the rest of this book if you're intending to pursue that route. The reason for that is understanding the process of bringing a book to print will help you navigate the industry as a whole.

If you're planning to self-publish, welcome back! Hopefully, the last chapter was at least interesting. If you skipped it entirely, well, here we are. One way or another, understanding this process will deepen your knowledge of our industry as a whole. For self-publishing authors, this information is vital and will help you navigate the process so you don't miss any steps.

The Elements of Publishing

The process of publishing a book, regardless of whether it's self-published or traditional publishing, has a few separate phases. What order things happen in will be partially a function of the publisher's personal flow of work, or yours, and the specifics of your book. I'm going to get deeper into the flow of work in the next section, but for now, I want to name the various parts that will go into publishing your book and both explain what they are and let you know more or less how they work.

To list them out, these are the categories of work that go into publishing a book:

- Editing
- Design (interior)
- Cover design
- Typesetting (also sometimes called "formatting" for ebooks)
- Distribution
- Marketing

Without further ado, let's get to explaining them.

Editing

Editing is more or less what you expect. Whether it's one round with an editor or multiple rounds with multiple editors will depend on your wallet or the publisher's flow of work. Most publishers do multiple rounds of editing, however. At minimum, they do a line edit and a copy edit followed by a proofread after formatting is complete, but typically, it will go through several rounds with at least two editors.

If you are self-publishing, editing will take on whatever form you choose to have it take, but I strongly suggest at least two rounds, one of line editing and one of copy editing, with two separate editors because different eyes catch different errors.

I will explain editing in more depth in the chapter about hiring editors, so don't think this is all I have to say on the subject. However, given that this is a whole chapter unto itself, I don't want to take up all the space by explaining it in full here.

Design (Interior)

This mostly happens for books where layout is not your standard novel layout. Non-fiction books, books with images and graphics, cookbooks, TTRPG (tabletop role-playing game) books, and so on. These are the kinds of books interior design becomes very important in. It can also include any custom break characters (scene or chapter) or images between chapters as some genres do. I consider writing your blurb to be part of this process, but it does require some special notes, so...

Blurb Writing

This is writing the back cover copy. It's a complicated beast that requires special training and study because copy writing is *not* the same as writing prose. It requires you to understand more about marketing than your average bear. If you're working with a publisher, they might either have a copywriter create it without your involvement or ask you to write up a short blurb and then have their in-house marketing people turn your initial write-up into a blurb.

I strongly suggest reading Bryan Cohen's *How to Write a Sizzling Synopsis*. It's an excellent book on the subject, and it provides far better and deeper insight into the process of creating one than I can in this overview.

Typesetting

This is the means through which a book is made to look like a book. If you're putting it out in print, the typesetter lays out the pages and ensures they all look good. It also means ensuring the frontmatter and backmatter are present, chapter headers look good, font choices, image placement... all those kinds of things.

There is a chapter coming that will provide a crash course for people wanting to do their own typesetting or those who just want to understand it better. During this process, or perhaps before, an ISBN will be assigned to the book.

ISBN Assignment

While self-published authors may or may not purchase an ISBN—you can have them assigned for free by many distributors—traditional publishers will purchase and assign them. The power of having an ISBN is it allows you to aggregate all your sales information for each format in one place, and you won't lose your "sales rank," so to speak, if you switch distributors.

When considering ISBNs, be aware that you will need a separate ISBN for each format, and some distributors get huffy if you use that ISBN to distribute with someone else (Amazon is notorious for this).

Distribution

If you're working with a traditional publisher, this isn't something you'll be involved in. However, if you're indie, you will need to decide what distributor(s) to go with and what methods. Again, we have a chapter on distribution in more detail.

Marketing

Marketing comes in two primary flavors when we're talking books. I'll be digging into marketing and advertising pretty hard in the chapters to come, but for now, you mostly need to know it's broken into two categories.

Pre-Release Marketing
This phase happens, as you might guess, before the book's launch and usually starts anywhere from three to six months prior to the release date.

Post-Release Marketing
Here we have the marketing period that happens after the book is released. It begins on launch day and continues until the end of time.

The Flow of Work

As with so many things in life, the order in which you do these things matters. If you have a cover designed before you know anything about your genre, you're going to miss steps. If you don't assign an ISBN until the day before your book launches, you're going to have a bad time getting everything to update before launch day.

While this flow of work differs from publisher to publisher and author to author, the rough outline of it more or less stays the same. I myself break this into three phases: book polishing, design and layout, and publishing preparation. The phases overlap a little, but they are distinct stages of the process and are performed in the order I laid out above.

Book Polishing

This phase is when the manuscript is cleaned up and prepared for publication. I am, at this point, assuming you have done all your self-editing and had beta readers review the work in question, so this is specifically past the point where you are engaging in those things.

This phase contains mostly the editing passes, which can be multiple, depending on the method you are using to publish. In a traditional publishing environment, this often includes several rounds of back-and-forth discussion with the author and editors.

Design and Layout

At this point, the manuscript is polished, and the other elements can be worked on. Often, the beginnings of cover design discussions and interior design discussions happen right toward the end of the last round of editing. Once the editing is done, the cover design and interior design pieces will be finalized, and layout will begin. Sometimes, layout may include discovering a need for interior design elements (text boxes, etc.), but usually, those decisions are made before typesetting begins.

Ebook formatting is done at the same time as typesetting, typically or done sequentially by the same person.

Publishing Preparation

This last phase overlaps some with the previous in the sense that, while the final pieces are put into place for the book itself, the ISBN is usually purchased and added to the typeset/formatted documents, and pre-release marketing begins. After the book itself is completed and prepared for publication, decisions about distribution are made, the marketing engine revs up, and then it's off to the races.

Realistic Timelines

Knowing now all the pieces that go into publishing a book, we should have a conversation about how long it is likely to take you to do all this work. I'm not going to go into the specifics of rapid release publishing strategies here because, while that can be a viable path for some people, I typically see it burn authors out in short order. There are books and courses on rapid release publishing, but if you are approaching writing as a long-term career, I advise against doing rapid release for long periods of time.

Certain projects, like this one, work fine for rapid release. I am putting this book and the first book in the set out at the same time, but that means I am writing, editing, and doing all the publication work for these ahead of time—in a timeline that is reasonable for me—and then releasing the books together. While the illusion is that I did all the work at the same time to make them available quickly, the reality is that I have been working on this pair of books for over a year to ensure they are ready for publishing, and that is as someone who has been in book publishing for around fifteen years. My pace is not your pace. Nor should it be. Your pace is your pace.

With that out of the way, let's talk realistic timelines.

In the traditional publishing world, the typical turnaround time for a book is between six months and a year. Some of that time will be them waiting for the right place in their publication schedule, but most of it will be solid work. Also, publishers like to have two or three months pre-release where the book is physically ready to go into print because certain review outlets require review copies months in advance before they will publish a review. On average, reviewers for pre-release reviews will want about a month of lead time.

For the purposes of this discussion, I am assuming the average-length novel (60k-85k) and that the book is going to the editor in clean condition. If the book requires deep, heavy edits, then it will require more passes and take longer. A publisher wouldn't accept a manuscript in that condition, but self-publishing authors may need to hire a developmental editor to do large-scale edits that require rewrites.

A single pass of editing can take between twenty and forty hours of active work, depending on the kind of editing and the length of the book. Most traditional publishers do several passes with time in between for the author to go over the edits and get them back to the editor. As a result, the editing process can sometimes take several months depending on how quickly you get your work back to the editor.

Editing is, by far, the heaviest lift of the publication process when it comes to time. The only part of the process that is more time-intensive is marketing, and the only piece more expensive is if you hire a cover artist to do an oil painting or some such thing. On average, however, editing is the bulk of the cost and time of publishing a book.

Typesetting a book varies in time depending on the complexity of the project, but it can take on average between a few days and a week to ensure the book is all set and ready to go. I am including proofreading in this time period since it happens along with typesetting. If you eschew hiring a typesetter and use software to do it yourself, it can be far faster, but I am laying this out presuming you are following the traditional publishing path.

The last phase doesn't take much in terms of time if you've made all your decisions, but I still strongly advise you to give yourself *at least* a month after the book is ready to print and even uploaded to distributors in order to do things like your cover reveal, pre-release hype, and preparing for launch day. I've seen authors not give themselves adequate lead time for this phase and end up with issues on launch day that hurt their sales significantly in ways that could have been avoided had they not rushed the process. Don't do that to yourself. Releasing a book is enough work and stress without you putting that kind of pressure on yourself.

Required Elements

Okay, while I don't advise skipping parts of the publication process, if you're self-publishing, you might not have the money to pay for all pieces of the publishing process as they "should" be done. I'll be going over some of the cost-cutting measures you can take in the chapters dedicated to the focal points, but I want to give you a list of things you can skimp on a little and some things you absolutely should not, as well as what is absolutely necessary in terms of doing business.

Things You Must Have

- Cover art
- Formatting for ebook
- Distribution
- A book blurb

Things You Should Have

- At least one pass with an editor (even if exclusively copy edits)
- Good-quality cover art
- An ISBN is strongly advised
- Typesetting (if producing a print copy) that is not done in Word

While I feel very, very strongly that having your book professionally edited is one of the deciding factors in success in your author career, I don't list it under "must" because you technically don't *need* it in order to put a book up for sale. Everything on the "must" list is absolutely required in order to sell the book, even if your entire plan is just to upload your novel to Amazon and do nothing else.

The other list is things I think are requirements but aren't technically necessary if you are going to do the bare minimum. The thing is, though, doing the absolute bare minimum is not the route to finding success in the long term. It might be necessary now and then in order to get going, but if you do nothing but the bare minimum, I guarantee you will end up with unsatisfying sales and angry reviews.

Summary

This chapter covers the flow of publishing whether you're doing it on your own or working with a publisher. The elements and steps are more or less the same either direction. Knowing the process will help you plan out your steps if you're self-publishing and have a rough idea of what's happening behind the curtain with a traditional publisher.

Not every author uses every single step of this process, but knowing all the various moving pieces provides you the ability to craft a flow of work that makes sense for your needs and your wallet if you are self-publishing. Traditional publishers, however, apply almost every step of the process to almost every book (assuming they are legitimate).

Key Takeaways

- Publishing, as a rule, has a predictable order of operations. It may vary a little here and there, but overall it follows that pattern in most publishers and for most self-publishing authors.

- While some of the pieces of the process may not be needed for every author every time, some elements are non-negotiable.

- Setting a realistic timeline and goal for yourself can help make sure you don't end up overly stressed or panicking while you try to get things done—particularly the first time.

- If you are self-publishing, developing a work flow that is repeatable and predictable will help you make sure you don't miss steps when you are publishing your books and can help you avoid many common pitfalls.

- Having an understanding of the publishing process will allow you to vet a traditional publisher by asking questions about their process or may give you a heads up when they are deviating from that usual flow of work. This can help you avoid scams and problems in the future.

Chapter Six

Purchasing Guide

In this chapter, I'm going to go over the things that you will want to look at and consider for purchases. Pricing may well change depending on when you purchase this book, so I'm not going to give dollar amounts if I can avoid it in this section. Instead, I will give you information about things you should consider purchasing and how, at the time of this publication, you go about getting them.

In addition, I want to cover why these items may be important to your book's lifetime and what service they are to you.

ISBNs

Let's start with the obvious question of what in the heck an ISBN is. If you open any book on your shelf or in your virtual library, you can find this number in the frontmatter. It's eleven or thirteen digits long and usually accompanied by the word ISBN. It also might be on the back cover somewhere in the vicinity of the barcode.

ISBN stands for "International Standard Book Number." To make that clearer, it functions essentially as your book's Social Security Number (SSN). It is a unique identifier for your book that nobody else has that allows you to track certain things about the book and allows purchasers to find it effectively.

If you are traditionally publishing, your publisher will handle this purchase—do not buy an ISBN if you are traditionally publishing this book. The reason for this is ISBNs are tied to the publisher. If you buy an ISBN yourself for your book and then approach a publisher, it will be wasted money because they will assign one to you.

In the United States, an ISBN can only be purchased from a company called Bowker. Individual ISBNs can get quite pricey, so I strongly recommend buying them in blocks to avoid having to spend an egregious sum of money. You will also need a separate ISBN for every format of the book *and* some distributors are sticky about allowing you to use an ISBN for an ebook if you distribute through other places. Amazon, for example, is notorious for this. They won't let you use an ISBN for an ebook if you have distributed the book through Draft2Digital or Ingram Spark for some reason.

This is a matter of frustration for the writing community at the moment because, in theory, it should be one ISBN, one format. Hopefully, by the time you read this, Amazon will have realized that policy is nonsense. The way I get around this personally is by having an ISBN assigned to the ebook and then using Amazon's free ISBN with the distribution on that platform. It's irksome, but it's just how it goes on there for now.

So, do you really *need* an ISBN?

That's a question that you're going to have to answer for yourself. Amazon and Draft2Digital will allow you to assign free ISBNs internally to your books with the downside being that, if you move your book to another distribution method, you cannot take that ISBN with you. So if I were to pull my book out of Amazon and move it to Ingram Spark, which *requires* an ISBN, the Amazon-assigned ISBN wouldn't go with it.

Also, if you intend to have your book available to bookstores and libraries, an ISBN is necessary for them to locate the book and order it. It is an important thing. However, if you have no interest in bookstore and library distribution and just intend on publishing your book in ebook format to Amazon, Barnes and Noble, Kobo, and Apple, etc., then you might not need one for your book.

You should also be aware that, if you release a new edition of your work, it will require a new ISBN. A "new edition" would be something like significant changes to the text—not just fixing typos but adding new chapters or rewriting significant swaths of text—changing the title, changing publishers, or if you're having your book translated into another language.

There are benefits to having an ISBN, but it's not an absolute necessity for every author and every book. I'm not listing this as a necessary purchase for that reason, but it is something you are going to need to evaluate for yourself.

Membership to Author Organizations

As with most professions, there are many author organizations out there that can provide a range of benefits from being more "professional" to having things like healthcare options for authors. Professional organizations can also help you network with other authors who may be farther ahead in their career than you are. It can also provide you opportunities to take courses, attend lectures, and find community.

While not every author needs to be part of one of these organizations, I would be remiss if I didn't mention their existence because they can provide valuable resources to authors looking to find their way in the field. Many of these organizations are geared toward specialty focuses, such as the Academy of American Poets, who specializes in—you got it—poetry. You also have the Science Fiction and Fantasy Writers Association (SFWA) and the International Association of Science Fiction and Fantasy Authors (IASFA).

Many of these organizations will vet their members to some degree and ensure that people joining them are legitimate. They also usually cost money to join, which means they weed out the less serious amongst us. I am currently a member of the Editorial Freelancers Association (EFA), Author Nation (AN) and the International Association of Sci-Fi and Fantasy Authors

(IASFA). The newsletters, networking, job listings in the EFA, and professional development courses are of significant and real value.

There are also organizations that focus on non-fiction or very specific types of writing such as public safety (Public Safety Writers Association), business writing (The Association of Business Journalists), journalism (Society of Professional Journalists) and so on. Whatever type of writing you are interested in doing or aspire toward, there are people who can help you on the step toward that goal.

Is it necessary to join one of these organizations to be a real writer? Of course not. You don't need to join an organization to be a professional, but you may find it helpful and useful to be on the inside of an organization who can help you and will provide you with access to information.

Book Awards

Okay, so let's get real for a moment. Book awards come in multiple flavors and levels of legitimacy. Also, anybody can call themselves an "award-winning author" if they won a writing competition in fifth grade. These terms are often thrown about, and while winning book awards can be a useful step toward a goal, it's not necessary.

It also may not even be particularly helpful, depending on the size of the award. There's a dramatic difference in winning a Pulitzer Prize and winning Grandma Gus's Hometown Author Award. It also comes with a price tag since most of these awards have an entry fee, and paying an entry fee may only be a good investment if you have an actual chance at winning and the prize itself is going to somehow help your career in a meaningful way.

Book awards on average charge between $50 and $200 to enter, so far as I know (at time of writing), and if that seems a little steep for something you might not actually win, it may not be a worthwhile investment. If you can throw money at it and not be damaged if you don't win, it could be a worthwhile endeavor.

If you're going to go the route of book awards, make sure you vet the award, make sure your book actually falls into the category of the award you're submitting to, and see what the requirements really are. Some awards require you to pay an entry fee and mail them a certain number of printed copies of the book, so it ends up being more than just the cost of the entry fee.

In some circles, having a book award or a nomination for one can help your cred. This is most prevalent in non-fiction since fiction readers care less about awards than they do about reading a damn good book. But in non-fiction, an award can be an indication that the contents of the book are accurate and well-researched, which is an important thing if you're going to someone for advice.

Having an award *can* certainly help people see your book. If it's a large or prestigious award, winning that award will put your name and book in front of a large audience who may purchase copies of your work as a result. It can also be a good ego boost and something to put on the wall behind you while you're filming TikTok videos. In addition, you can put the fact that you won that award anywhere you put the book. It can feel really good if you fight with imposter syndrome.

The thing is, though, winning an award probably isn't going to translate into sales unless you win a really big award. As such, whether or not you should try for them is going to be mostly a function of how much money you have to spend on it, whether or not you think the bragging rights is worth it, and if you believe it is going to be something of personal importance to you as an author.

The Costs of Doing Business

As I've mentioned earlier on, the costs of doing business are not nothing. I'm going to give you a list of average prices you can look at to consider the real brass tacks costs behind purchasing different book services. As much as I don't want to put dollar amounts into a book that's set at a fixed time, I think it's important to give you some kind of starting point.

I cannot speak for all editors, so instead of trying, I will give you very rough estimates of how much various services would cost from me on a book that is *65,000 words long and is relatively clean.* "Clean" meaning I don't need to stop every few words to make a correction, and the manuscript doesn't look like it's bleeding to death when I'm done editing it. I prefer to charge by the word versus by the hour for reasons relating to my personal quirks, but if I look at something and see that it is going to be a tremendously heavy edit, my cost per word will go up from the baseline because it will result in me having to take far more time. And, as we all know, time is money.

Using the above criteria, here is a list of rough estimates of what I charge clients for the various services I provide as of the time of writing this book. Editors have to adjust prices to account for inflation like everyone else, and with the cost of living being high right now, that's an unfortunate reality we have to pass along to clients if we want to do fancy things like eat food and have electricity. You know, the luxuries in life.

Costs for Editing

- Manuscript Analysis: $455
- Developmental Edits: $1,300
- Line Edits: $1,625
- Copy Edits: $975
- Proof Reading: $650

Other Services

- Print Typesetting: $975
- Ebook formatting: $50
- Book Coaching: $60/hr, $40/half hr (half hour minimum)
- Cover Design: $250 - $1,500+ (photo manipulation vs. hand-painted artwork)
- Mapmaking: $250 - $1,500+ (watercolor by hand, varies by size and complexity)
- ISBN (Bowker): $125 for one, $295 for 10

Keep in mind that my rates reflect my industry experience, my study, my overhead costs of doing business, and the value I bring to my work. There are many editors who charge more than I do, and there are many who charge less. Pricing is a rather personal thing for editors, and there is also a divide between those who work in non-fiction fields and those who work in fiction.

If you want to get an idea of what rates can look like across the spectrum, I strongly suggest you visit the Editorial Freelancers Association website and check out their Editorial Rates page. It has data from a large swath of professional editors of different stripes and experience levels. Keep in mind the pricing is the median pricing, which means there are outliers on either side, and the rates page is a reference. It reflects the rates editors charge; it doesn't set them.

Make sure you look for updated costs of doing business for the time you're reading this, however. Also, recognize that these costs are based on having a professional of some level of skill doing these things for you. You absolutely can find cheaper prices, but you run the risk of buying the editing equivalent of a "Rolex" from a guy in a trench coat on a street corner. This is not to say that you cannot find good quality professionals who work for less money—you absolutely can. However, services that are dramatically cheaper deserve some serious side eye before you pay for them.

If you're unsure if an editor, typesetter, or other professional is worth the money you are being asked to pay, it is perfectly reasonable to vet them. Ask if they have testimonials, any clients you can contact to ask questions, and see if they have social cred. Also, see if they have any professional memberships, such as to the EFA or CIEP or other editing organizations. Not all professionals are members of those organizations, so it's not an immediate indication of someone who isn't a professional. However, if they *are* a member of those organizations, it can help provide some certainty that you are working with someone who takes this profession seriously.

Paid Book Reviews

Okay, so I want to put this out there for everyone who is reading this. Paid book reviews are typically the work of scam artists. There are a few legitimate outlets that charge money, and we'll get into that, but if you ask someone to review your ARC or your book, and they ask you for money, walk away. Immediately.

To be clear here, when I say "review," I don't mean someone providing editorial feedback. I mean people writing a book review on Amazon, Goodreads, or other platform. This is not an edit, and these people are not expected to be professionals.

Part of the reason is that, if you pay for a review, and that review is posted to Amazon (by the reviewer in the review section, not an editorial review), that is immediately cause for Amazon to remove your account and kick you out of their system. No second chances. No questions. It's firmly against their TOS. There *is* a section of your book where you can share editorial reviews, such as from journals, etc., and *those* can be paid for. But we will get into the difference in a minute.

Recently, there has been a group of people on certain social media apps being angry that authors want them to do ARC reads for free and thinking authors should pay for their time. The cold, hard reality is that we cannot. An ARC read or review is compensated by the reviewer receiving a free copy of the book, which is not worth nothing, as well as whatever goodies come in a book box to that reviewer, assuming a physical copy. ARC readers and reviewers are usually not professionals unless they work for a large review outlet. We will talk about that in a minute, though.

Quite frankly, if you do solicit a review from someone who is big in your field, and they give you one? It's liquid gold. However, I can't pay Jim Butcher to read my book series and give me a gold star. (Though, Jim, if you ever read this, I will totally take head pats, gold stars, and I will mail you cookies or something. Please review my books? Puppy eyes!)

Furthermore, unless the individual providing the review has the capacity to make that review actually sell books, they don't deserve to be paid money. Book reviews are important, and they are valuable. I love the reviewers who take time to write reviews on my books and series, and I appreciate them. But unless they're Neil himself, a single review from "Bobby R." on Amazon isn't going to sell books by itself. A lot of reviews will help the algorithm see my novels and help me gain traction, but one review from someone who isn't a celebrity isn't going to do a lot directly.

Which brings me to paid reviews.

There *are* legitimate paid reviewers out there. Kirkus Reviews is one of the biggest ones in the business. There are also literary magazines, newspapers, and other outlets who will review your book for money. In the case of those situations, what you are paying for is the book review being published and/or syndicated to other publications. Their stamp of approval on a book actually means something, and having it allows you access to marketing channels and/or will give you professional clout. Kirkus also has a magazine that goes out to a large number of people and industry influencers. As such, the price tag for their review (about $450) is reasonable if you are at the point in your career where that makes financial sense for you.

However.

Early on in your career, before you have books out and if your book is not of equal quality to something that would be published by Penguin/Random House, it's not worth the expense. You would likely receive a bad review because you're not paying for good reviews; you're paying for eyes on, and then it would be a waste of a lot of money.

You will also note that everything I said above? None of that includes posting the review to Amazon or Goodreads. Bigtime literary reviewers like Kirkus don't do that. You would, instead, put their review in the "editorial reviews" section of your page. It's the same with literary magazines and other review outlets of this caliber. If you are going to throw money at reviews—and when you're very early on in your career, I don't advise it—you should stick to outlets like Kirkus Book Reviews, The New York Times Book Review, or other such established professionals.

Book reviews are important, and we're going to talk a little more about getting them later on when I talk about marketing, but I wanted to put out there that paying for them from anyone but people who are the peers of Kirkus is a scam, and you shouldn't be duped by people trying to drag money from you. Don't give in because unless they are a big author, a well-known influencer, the New York Times Review of Books, or something similar, their opinion won't move the needle enough to justify paying for it.

Summary

There are a number of things you can buy when it comes to your publishing career. Some are optional and can be trimmed if you are unable to purchase them while others are not really negotiable if you want to have a professional quality product. This chapter covered a number of those items, where to buy them, and what you actually *need* versus what might be helpful or beneficial but can be done without.

Key Takeaways

- Having a solid understanding of what you must spend money on and what you can perhaps trim is a necessary thing when making business decisions for yourself. It can also help you save up for certain elements of the process, depending on which pieces you choose to purchase.

- How you choose to spend your money as an author can vary and grow over time. What might be out of reach or not make sense for you to purchase now may make sense in a few years. Understanding where you are in your career will help you identify what you can and should spend money on.

Chapter Seven

Working with Professionals

This is something I come across a lot: people who have no idea how to work with professionals in the writing space. It's very different than working with a book club or exchanging beta reads in a Facebook group with your peers. Knowing how to approach a professional and work with one is a vital skill.

Since many authors don't come from a background where they are sure how to handle a professional in their writing space, this chapter will cover that. However, at the ground level, most professionals should be treated similar to how you'd treat a doctor or mechanic. Their expertise comes from a long history of study and work, and while you might need a second opinion or to change practices, there's usually logic behind what they suggest.

Hiring someone to work on your book is likely to be uncomfortable the first few times, so accepting that early will help you get a jump on managing those feelings.

Why Hiring Professionals Makes a Difference

While I don't feel like I need to explain this to most of you by this point, I'm going to do it anyway. Hiring professionals matters. I know there's a lot of "wisdom" in writing groups about how you can cut corners and get away with avoiding us. It's rife in the self-publishing world because professionals aren't cheap. Unfortunately, that advice is not going to get you to where you need to be.

If you're looking to produce quality products, you need to hire quality people.

Think of it this way: Would you be more inclined to accept business advice from someone with an MBA who has worked in the field for years, or from someone who reads the Wall Street Journal sometimes? Because that's the difference. One individual has credentials, deep knowledge, and industry experience. The other has feelings and has developed opinions based on half a story without possessing the education to understand the context or evaluate whether or not what they read is even accurate.

Professionals will also be straight with you. They're not going to pull punches and tell you something's good when it's not. However, they *will* provide you solid, evidence-based ways to fix the problem and be able to explain exactly what the problem is.

Another thing professionals bring to the table is an understanding of your genre and your market. Given that I am primarily focused on editing the kinds of books I enjoy reading, I know what's out there and what sells. I know what the expectations of the readers are. An expert cover designer knows the trends happening in your genre right now and can ensure your book meets those trends while *also* standing out enough to be unique and draw the eye. Experience and knowledge of the target market are items of significant value. Particularly if you, the author, are new to publishing and don't quite have all that nailed down yet.

Professional editors are also often experts in fields beyond just the written word. For example, I specialize in fantasy and bring into that my knowledge of swordplay (I'm a historical European fencer and taught Kenjutsu—Japanese sword—for years) and martial arts. I bring my understanding of textiles and fabrics. I bring my knowledge of sumptuary laws and different kinds of governance structures. My degree in European history opens doors for me to know what words, technologies, and other things were around in that time period. This, of course, means I can save my authors from unintentionally having anachronistic things in their sword-and-sorcery novels. I also have a solid understanding of mythology across the world and can use that to help authors flesh out their worlds a little more. These are only a few of the things I come equipped with if you choose me as your co-pilot. I also understand mental health, police procedure, medicine and injuries, and a whole host of other subjects I can talk your ear off about forever.

My point here is that, when you hire a professional, you not only hire them for their expertise in just the thing you want them to do, they bring with them a whole trunk full of useful and interesting knowledge and tidbits that flow into and around their work and influence their understanding. That kind of thing adds value.

This is not to say non-professionals don't have life experience. Of course they do. Everybody does. However, not everyone knows how to leverage that life experience into writing, editing, cover design, marketing, and so on. Pairing those areas of knowledge and life experience with expertise in their sphere is invaluable in a teammate.

Working with a professional can also help alleviate a lot of the fear. A large portion of my job is helping my clients believe in themselves and in their work. Even if I'm making their manuscript bleed, I am *also* identifying the good things in their work and helping them see past imposter syndrome. I also work with people who have no idea what the heck they're going to *do* with a manuscript once it's edited, so I talk them through their options, and we discuss what might be best for them. Which is, honestly, what led me to writing this book. While my advice here is less specifically personal, it's the same conversation I've been having over and over again for the last sixteen years. I might as well write it down and share it.

Where to Find Professionals

We've talked about how there are sharks in our water repeatedly through this book, so this time, we're going to take a different angle and help you find places where the folks who aren't sharks congregate and how you can identify and locate us.

There are many places you can find professionals to work with, and trying to list them all would be both futile and result in this work being out of date very quickly. However, I can refer you to a few that should be useful long into the future.

The first ones I'm going to nod to are professional organizations. Many of the various organizations have mailing lists and/or directories where you can find their members. This includes places like the EFA, CIEP, and so on. There are editing groups on Facebook, and there's the website Reedsy, which has listings. You can even find us on Fiverr, though *caveat emptor* there—make sure you vet people. We are often found in flocks on social media, clucking about our areas of expertise.

We also usually have websites that will show information about what we do, what our credentials are, and often a list of books we've worked on. No matter where you find an editor, you should be able to ask them for more information and have them be glad to show you things. That said, be aware that not all editors can give you lists of authors they've worked with. There are times when we sign agreements that prevent us from disclosing things (frequently seen with ghostwriting work, for example).

Professional cover artists are found in similar places to professional editors. We are all over the place online, and cover artists can be vetted through portfolios.

When it comes to professional marketing assistance, you can see what information they offer, what their rates are, and what they promise.

Generally speaking, professionals don't message or email authors asking to work on their novel without being made aware you're looking. If you post in a writing group that you're looking for an editor, and one DMs you, that's not an immediate red flag. If you post that you're writing a book, and someone slides into your DMs to try and sell you services, that's the problem.

Unsolicited DMs might be a newbie who doesn't know the proper way to handle clients or who is trying to start out with clients. Or it could be a shark claiming to be something they're not. If you ask questions, and the person is honest about being a newbie, then it's up to you whether you want to work with them. If they provide the services you want at a price point that works for you, and you're all right with the fact that they are just entering the business, then there's nothing wrong with that.

On the flip side, if someone approaches you making promises about selling certain numbers of books, promises that you'll be picked up and published by big publishers, or says that you should give them money to tweet about your book to their audience of a million bots on X (Twitter), you should decline. Those are scam artists looking to prey on authors.

Care and Feeding of Professionals

The first thing I want to underline here is to reiterate something I touched on earlier: Professionals aren't your enemy. We are, in fact, your teammates, your cheering squad, and your coach all rolled into one. No professional will take umbrage to being vetted, but remember that we aren't trying to crawl out of your screen to demand your book like that girl from the movie *The Ring*.

With that in mind, please know we are here to help. This means no question is too stupid. If you need something clarified, you can ask; we only are going to judge your grammar when we're being paid. I regularly receive friendly, chatty, or anxious messages and emails from clients, and while some editors prefer to operate at more arm's length, I have no problems building that bubble.

One of the things professionals will appreciate immensely is if you come to them with the information they need right off the bat. They'll be pleased and impressed because it will smooth the workflow and allow them to give you the best and fastest service.

Depending on what service you're asking for, the information they need will differ, but here are a few possibilities.

- Editing: Word count, genre, what type of editing you think you might want, germane content warnings (don't worry about spoilers with us)

- Typesetting: Word count, trim size, any interior design elements you want to put in place

- Cover Design: Page count (typeset), trim size, back cover blurb, genre, covers that are comparable to what you would like, a description of what you think you might want

- Marketing: Any plans you've come up with, your social media handle(s), a link to your website, what your goals are, and where you are in the publishing process

Those are some of the professionals you might work with and what information they'll need in order to proceed. Now, it's okay if you don't know yet what all those things are. If you aren't entirely sure what answer to give for some of that, like trim size, it's okay to ask. In fact, we fully expect you to ask, and many of us have responses to our most commonly asked questions that we keep in our metaphorical back pocket at all times.

As an aside, trim size is the physical size of the book. I'll explain more about that in detail when we get to the typesetting chapter.

If, and maybe when, you disagree with the professional you hired, remember that we're humans. Also, a true professional will fully recognize and respect that your book is *your* book, not theirs. We may have some very strong advice on certain points—particularly when dealing with things relating to sensitivity reading—and part of our job is giving you the benefit of our expertise. That said, we understand that the ultimate decision is up to you whether or not you listen to us.

The exception to that is if you are working with a publisher and their in-house team. At that point, the team you are working with has the right to make the final call because they are employees of the publisher, not you. By that point, you have signed a contract giving them the right to do that. Not to say they won't treat your work with respect (we hope), but since the publisher is the client whose reputation is on the line, they have certain guidelines and parameters they have to adhere to, and their word is often law in certain things.

If you do want to push back on some advice a professional has given you or work they have done, please do so in a respectful way. You're allowed to disagree and discuss things within reason. However, if you email me about every single comma change in your manuscript, I may have to hold you upside down and shake you. If you feel a professional has misunderstood something, you can also explain it to them, and perhaps they will adjust their advice or work accordingly.

If you are self-publishing, you don't need to argue with your professionals. You can just reject their changes and move on with your life unless you want further clarification. I don't advise ignoring our advice flippantly because our job is to help you make your book the best it possibly can be. However, if you feel strongly about something, you are allowed to ignore us. It may be a very expensive mistake, depending on the advice received, but nonetheless, you have that right.

As a general rule, when you work with most professionals, there is a contract of some kind in place to protect both parties. These contracts will have clauses determining when and how you can terminate work within the scope of the project. They will also lay out the exact scope of work provided and what rights you have and what rights the hired professional has. Some professionals eschew contracts but produce exemplary work, but most of us who have been in the trenches for awhile will insist on at least a simple agreement with the outline of terms, payment, and rights.

Should you be working with a professional who doesn't have a contract, you are not out of bounds to ask for one.

Book Professional Myth Busting

It can be intimidating to send your manuscript off to a relative stranger to be torn apart or to work with a cover designer on your book. The whole process can be very expensive and leave you feeling raw, worried, and vulnerable. My primary clientele base is new authors or authors who were new when they started with me. I have fielded many a fearful message about whether or not I hate them or their book.

To help you allay those fears, I want to lay out some of the things you can expect from professionals in the literary sphere. I find that de-mystifying the process helps ease worries because it removes the unknown aspect of the interaction.

Professional editors aren't going to steal your book.

Editors are on the inside of the industry. We know exactly how much work and money it costs to take a book from manuscript to print because we deal with it on the daily. We also know how hard marketing can be and how long it can take to turn a profit on books. As such, why would we steal your book when you're already paying us?

Those editors who are also authors like myself don't need to lift others' ideas to produce books. I have plenty of my own and have no interest in spending the amount of time it would take to polish something that isn't mine. Not to mention doing so would result in the swift end of our careers. Regardless of my morality on the subject, I want editing to be my profession for a good, long time. If I steal people's books, I will be destroying my ability to do that.

As a final note to this topic, I refer you to the segment about contracts. My contract covers the fact that I will not sell, republish, or otherwise share any work that is given to me by a client. That's one of the reasons contracts are valuable.

We are likely to be direct and honest about what we think.

When I say "direct," I don't intend that to be code for "mean." I can be forthright without being unkind. However, you are hiring me to give you real, genuine, honest feedback. That's my job. My expertise is why you wanted to come to me to begin with, and if I'm not giving you true feedback, *I'm not giving you your money's worth.*

Be aware that our job is to point out the weak points, correct the errors, and fix the spots that need fixing. Just like you don't go to a mechanic when your car is running perfectly (unless you are having an inspection done or need an oil change), you don't go to an editor and expect your book is perfect, either. Heck, sometimes, you think you just need an oil change, and it turns out you need major work on something you didn't realize was a problem.

Your professional, however, should provide this feedback kindly. We need to be direct and honest, but if your editor talks down to you, calls you names, mocks you, or otherwise makes you feel bad beyond the fact that editing is HARD to take sometimes, then it's a problem. If this is a problem you have, then communicate with your editor about it. It's possible they didn't intend to come across that way, and they may be able to help you feel better. Or, if they're a jerk, it's time to look at the exit clauses in your contract.

While this is fully anecdotal, I have also noticed an above-average number of autistic people drawn to the profession of editing. That is of no surprise, given our pattern recognition skills, enjoyment of special interest, and delight in clear rules and guidelines. If you are working with an autistic person, there's a good chance we may be more direct than you expect. It's never an attempt to be mean, but I acknowledge that it does sometimes sting.

We don't judge typos in your emails or messages.

The line I come back to again and again whenever someone apologizes for a typo in a message or email is this: "I only judge when I'm being paid to." Generally speaking, no matter how anal retentive we are when we are working on a manuscript, we aren't like that in daily life. I just don't have the energy for it, personally. While I might be a little picky about sharing memes with glaring errors in them, I don't sit around correcting my friends' grammar.

I also have editor friends with whom, in DMs, we talk like complete fools, and there isn't a single ounce of grammar to be seen. We know what we're talking about, however, and we're having a grand old time. This might come as a shock to some folks, but we are whole, entire people whose affection for grammar and punctuation doesn't usually come with snootiness about it unless you really wind us up and get us going about why so much of what we learned in high school is dead wrong.

We'll have *feelings* about that.

Not all professionals provide regular or frequent updates.

I know some editors who provide clockwork updates on where they are in a project. I know some who go dark, crawl into their editing cave, and shut the doors until they're finished and talk to exactly *no one*. We all have our own process. If you want to know where a project is, it's okay to ask for information at a reasonable interval. Keep in mind that every day is not a reasonable interval for most editors. However, once a week from the start date of your project is not an unfair ask.

Cover designers and artists are the same. Some artists show regular in-progress shots while others provide progress updates only at points where you have both agreed that you can request changes (typically: sketch phase, line art phase, flat color phase, finished color phase, typography phase). It's not unreasonable to ask for some information if it's been a while without any information, but you should also ensure that you aren't pestering them constantly because it will break their focus. (Cue the video clip from *Monsters Inc.* about the two interns arguing about making Sully lose his focus.)

We cannot read your mind.

What I mean by this is, if you have questions or concerns about the direction of something, it is always better to talk to the person you have hired rather than wait until they are finished and produce something you are not satisfied with.

We also don't always know what you want if you don't give us that insight, so make sure you keep an open and clear line of communication with your professional!

You are absolutely allowed to tell us if you don't like something, too. We may disagree on it, and we might need to talk it through, but the only way we can do that is if you tell us! After all, our psychic powers are limited to telepathically sending other editors stupid memes. And now you know our secret.

We are going to be very serious about avoiding "scope creep."

"Scope creep" is when a project's goalposts keep moving. This means springing things on us that aren't in the original agreement, requests or expectations that we are going to re-edit work for free, or expecting free work on large swaths of text.

This is not to say the parameters of a project cannot change, but if you want them to change, you need to let the professional know and then renegotiate the contract, and pay them adequately for their time.

All of us have had horror story experiences where clients have wanted more and more from us without being willing to pay for the extra time and work. This can include things like being peppered with phone calls or emails that take time to respond to—and that time adds up—an author rewriting portions of the book while we are editing a draft and then expecting us to edit new parts of it, clients asking for more complex and detailed art than was initially agreed upon, etc.

With that in mind, we are likely to be quick to step back if we get the idea that you're heading in that direction. We are not unfriendly or unwilling to give you a little extra time, like a phone call to help talk you off a metaphorical ledge after your edits come back and you are worried we hate you. Just make sure you know that, when you are contacting us, that is working time you aren't being billed for, and unless the professional has consented to that arrangement, it can quickly become a lot of work time that takes us away from other projects and clients.

Some professionals absolutely will never talk to you on the phone.

There are a lot of us who are entirely against the idea of taking phone calls from clients. This can be caused by many reasons, none of which are about you personally.

I know many editors who have autism, ADHD, or other such conditions who don't do phone calls well and find them incredibly anxiety-inducing. There as many professionals who want everything in writing because they've had legal problems in the past and absolutely demand a paper trail after that. There are professionals who feel it is a waste of their time when they are able to get all the work done via email.

Requesting a phone call or video conference is a reasonable ask, particularly if they haven't told you they don't do them. However, don't be surprised if they decline, and please don't pressure for it. Many of us are far more comfortable with text, and while we respect that some clients find phone calls a better way to "get to know us," we are frequently skittish beasties. Just know that being declined to do a phone call or video chat isn't personal.

Asking us to sign an NDA immediately is usually a red flag.

There are very, very few exceptions to this, and those exceptions include things like books about ongoing court cases, works that contain industry or trade secrets, or other such things. If you are hiring someone to edit a work of fiction, asking them to sign an NDA off the bat will immediately set their feelers waving.

It's not that we sit around behind closed doors sending each other client manuscripts because we absolutely do no such thing. In fact, editors are extremely respectful of authors' manuscripts on the whole. The most we will do is share a sentence with colleagues in private if we're struggling to figure out if the punctuation is right or if we're sleep deprived.

The reason this is a red flag is because it shows the author has no idea how intellectual property laws work and indicates that they are a complete newbie on the scene. As mentioned earlier in the segment where I was talking about how we aren't going to steal your book, this applies for the same reasons. We aren't going to steal your ideas because it would be outrageously expensive to do so.

Furthermore, editors typically have clauses in their contracts that cover such things already, so signing a separate NDA is overkill outside of the above stipulations. Artists typically aren't reading the book, either, so having *them* sign an NDA is overkill. Their contracts will include things about where and when and how art can be displayed. Also note that, unless you specifically pay for it, *you* do not own the copyright to your cover images; the artist retains those unless you pay for them. They are just granting you license.

Addressing the Cost Problem

Professional help is expensive. That is true in all spheres of life, and it's no less true here. When it comes to publishing, if you cannot afford professional help, you might want to consider going traditional. Or, if you are unwilling to go traditional but unable to pay a professional their full, earned wage, you can learn how to do some things yourself.

It is entirely possible to learn to typeset and do graphic design on your own. If you have the time and interest, you can spend a lot of time on YouTube learning all the various different skills that come together to replace a lot of these professionals you would hire. You cannot *replace* an editor, but you certainly can learn a great deal about writing and use the available tools out there to help.

Things like Hemingway, Grammarly, ChatGPT (*caveat emptor* on that one), ProWritingAid, PerfectIt, SmartEdit, and any number of tools will help you refine and edit your text pretty dang well if you take the time and do the study you need to in order to produce good-quality writing. You can also spend time on the Purdue OWL and take their grammar quizzes and classes for free.

There *are* cheaper options out there, and there are even some pretty decent cover designers out there who will work for extremely cheap because they live in countries where the cost of living is lower than in the United States. You need to vet those folks, though, and make sure your cover artist has rights to use the fonts and images in question or else you can end up in legal hot water.

The thing is, though, there are no shortcuts. You either pay someone with knowledge and experience you don't have, or you learn how to do the work and take the time to do it. There's no escaping that. It's just like keeping your house clean. Either you hire a cleaning service and pay them to do the work, or you do your own dishes and vacuuming. There is no in between if you want to be successful.

Anybody claiming to have shortcuts that will help you avoid either learning on your own or paying a professional is a shill. There *is* software out there to help with some of it, but they're not a shortcut so much as they are a tool. I'll be getting into those in detail in the chapters that address them, but I am just trying to underline yet again that there's no cheap, fast, and good-quality way forward with publishing as a whole, though there are some pieces of software to help with typesetting that automate the process to some extent. It's either fast and good, cheap and fast, or good and cheap. You never get all three.

I reiterate that, if you absolutely cannot afford to invest in your work on a financial level, you should give deep and serious consideration to going the traditional route. Yes, it means delayed gratification and a loss of a certain degree of creative control. Yes, it means a lot of rejection and uncertainty. But it also might be the most realistic solution for your situation.

Also, if you *are* going the traditional route, the next three chapters are going to mostly be interesting information you don't necessarily need to know the details of since you will have a team doing this for you. However, being aware of what goes into it is always a useful thing, so I don't advise you skip them entirely!

Summary

As an author, you are likely going to encounter and work with many professionals in your writing journey. Building your team is an art form unto itself, and knowing how to handle that team is necessary. Fortunately, most professionals understand newbie errors and are very forgiving of an author who doesn't know all the steps of the dance yet. Just treat us with the same respect you'd treat anyone else, and you are unlikely to run into issues!

Key Takeaways

- Hiring professionals to undertake elements of your process can both save you money and frustration. It can also ensure your book is ready for public consumption!

- Finding professionals can feel daunting, but there are many places you can look for vetted individuals to work with, including professional organizations, websites that list individuals, and author organizations.

- Working with a professional doesn't need to be something you fear. We won't eat you! Be respectful, kind, and considerate, and we will do the same. If you don't understand something, ask. Asking questions is not a faux pas by any stretch of the imagination.

- There are a ton of myths surrounding working with a professional of any type, and there's a lot of anxiety around—particularly when it comes to editors. Remember that we are just people like you, and if you are hiring one of us, we are working in your favor and want your book to succeed.

- Working with professionals is not cheap. It comes with a price tag, and that can be a high one. There are ways you can lower costs by ensuring you get us the right information and are prepared for the process, but it is not typically inexpensive.

- If you cannot afford to hire professionals, yourself, giving consideration to traditional publishing is an important thought. It will provide you access to people with deep knowledge without having to invest your life's savings into it.

Chapter Eight

Hiring an Editor

We talked in the last chapter about working with professionals for a while, but in this one, I am going to dig into the specifics of finding an editor and working with one. This is the area in which I have the most expertise because this is what I do professionally.

Editing can look like a lot of things, and while you may think you know what's up with it, I still advise taking a stroll through this chapter to make sure you have a strong understanding. Many people don't realize there are many types of editing out there with different focuses, and as a result, they end up hiring the wrong person for the job or enter into a contract not realizing it's not what they wanted.

The Types of Editing

If you are coming from the previous book in this series, you've already read my explanation on this subject, so you will be hearing me re-tread old ground. However, this is information vital to knowing who to contact and how to proceed with publishing a book, so I am just going to sally forth and explain it again.

The list below is in the order of operation and includes some things not *technically* editing but editing-adjacent and are services editors may or may not offer in addition to various types of editing. Also be aware that not all editors do all types of editing!

Finally, not all editors define these types of editing exactly the same way. There are places that define what I call "line editing" as "heavy copy editing" or sometimes "substantive editing." Others exchange "developmental editing" and "substantive editing." That doesn't help any with clearing up confusion, I know, but I'd be remiss if I didn't at least mention it as a reality you could come across in the world.

Book Coaching

This is one of those editing-adjacent services I mentioned that some editors provide but isn't technically editing. Book coaching is designed to help with the process of writing. You can communicate with a book coach at any stage of writing if you get stuck or need guidance on what to do next. They can help you with your outline, help you plan your book, help you work out a plot snarl, help you figure out your mid-book doldrums, or give you some guidance on the process of publishing. They may also be a person with expertise in your specific area of non-fiction and be able to offer insight into where to find information you need, how to approach difficulties, and help you find your target market, which will help you know who you're writing *to*.

I do book coaching, and this service is always tailored to what my client needs at any given time. If they need me to help them organize their plot, that's what we do. If they need me to help them with their world building, we do that. I'm up to my elbows in their book with them. Sometimes, it's just a single session to help them put their thoughts together. Other times, it's weekly or monthly meetings to help them stay accountable. It can be a lot of things, but in essence, this kind of coaching is having an expert help you connect the dots of whatever it is you're dealing with. If this sounds like something you'd find helpful, please feel free to contact me, and we can set up some time to work through things together.

Manuscript Assessment

Again, this is an editing-adjacent service. It's not deep enough that I'd call it actual editing, but it is one of the least expensive services editors offer. Unlike developmental edits, the goal of this is to provide a high-level read through and offer you some limited feedback on things you need to look at.

This advice comes in the form of an editorial letter, which is something most forms of editing come with, that addresses these items. However, unlike developmental editing, the editor is unlikely to do comments in the manuscript or provide deep and complete feedback. To provide an example, I have done developmental edits that have had nearly 10,000-word editorial letters breaking down the good, the bad, and the ugly. Manuscript assessments get around 1,000 words.

If that sounds like a rip off, remember that you are still receiving an average of 8-10 hours of that professional's time and a distillation of what they notice. It's not as robust as a developmental edit, but it will give you direction and provide you with recommendations. It can also be used as a tool to help an editor determine what type of editing you truly need instead of finding out halfway through a line edit that you need a developmental edit instead.

Developmental Editing

This form of editing is the second most expensive I offer and is one I primarily recommend to authors who are still learning their craft. The focus of developmental editing is the broad strokes items like plot structure, characterization, pacing, world building, research, and the other things that can result in chapters being deleted, rewritten, or otherwise moved around.

Developmental editing is also the first "actual" editing step. It usually includes comments in the margins of the manuscript and a deep editorial letter. I cannot speak for other editors, but I also do an outline of what is in the manuscript when I receive it along with an in-depth editorial letter that discusses the big picture items in the manuscript that need working on.

Line Editing

Line editing is my specialty. While I love developmental, line is the type I find the most rewarding. It deals with cleaning the prose to a mirror shine. Your editor will help you tighten up your book and round off all the rough edges. To be more specific about it, this is where we work the deepest on the craft of writing itself. Word choice, sentence structure, descriptions, removing excess fluff, and cutting down into the heart of things. Part of this process is elevating the author's voice and clarifying it to both be the most *them* it can be as well as refining it to be enjoyable to readers.

With line editing comes comments in the margins, tracked changes to show where edits were made, and an editorial letter discussing the craft elements and highlighting any places the author needs help or focus on. The editorial letter for line editing is far shorter than that of a developmental edit since the bulk of the work is done in the manuscript itself.

It is also the most expensive type of editing as a general rule. It often takes the most time on the part of the editor because they must evaluate every single word of the manuscript for appropriateness and accuracy.

Copy Editing

When I do a line edit, I naturally fold a copy edit into it. However, doing copy edits alone is absolutely a skill many editors possess. Copy edits are focused on grammar, syntax, spelling, clarity, and punctuation. It also encompasses things like consistency of spelling (toward vs. towards, for example).

You will likely receive an editorial letter with this type of editing, but it will be focused on the scope of copy editing and cover things relating to that. It also may include notes the editor took while reviewing your book that fall outside the scope of their edit if they have any recommendations.

Proofreading

Many people misunderstand proofreading as the final glance over something before it goes to publication on a generic level. This is untrue. In the purest sense, this is the last step, taken *after* the work is formatted for print. A proofreader is looking exclusively for things relating to formatting or correcting minor typographical errors. They will review things like fonts and styles being correctly applied, headings all being set up properly, identifying text flow and pagination issues, and making sure the front- and backmatter are in the places they belong. In ebooks, this includes things like checking out the table of contents and so on as well.

Proofreading doesn't typically come with an editorial letter unless it needs a list of issues found and fixed. Most of the time, it is done in Adobe InDesign, or Affinity Publisher, or Adobe Acrobat Pro because this individual is working on an already formatted work. If proofreading is performed on an ebook, it may be done in Word since ebook formatting prior to conversion is usually done in Word.

Why Editing is So Expensive

This segment isn't so much me trying to sell you on something as it is trying to explain some key elements of the business people often don't think about. The first is that editing is costly not only because of the editor's time, experience level, and expertise, but also because editing comes with overhead. In order to do our jobs, we rely on electricity, internet, subscription software, professional organization memberships, professional training, website costs, ergonomic office furniture to protect us from repetitive motion injuries and issues with posture, computers, and all the rest. All those things add up over time.

Unless you are working with a publisher, editors are also typically freelancers. This means we are also responsible for our own insurance costs, which are expensive in the U.S., and taxes above and beyond personal taxes if we have an LLC or other company.

There's a misconception that editors are also "just reading" in some cases. While it's true we are reading the book, we are also assessing every single word like a targeting computer. It is hard, heavy brain work that requires intense attention because losing focus means missing errors. Our job requires us to be present and focused at all times, and we cannot "check out" to do it. That means long stretches of deep and intensive focus.

I often refer to my job as being a "book mechanic" because I equate the two spheres. While one is purely intellectual and academic and the other has a lot more physical elements to it, both editing and being a mechanic require trained skills, specialized tools, and specific knowledge, as well as the ability to do problem solving of different types. If the mechanic is in business for themselves, they have to buy the tools, pay rent on the location, and handle the overhead of doing business.

Editors aren't attempting to gatekeep and prevent anyone without deep pockets from entering the publishing sphere. We truly aren't. However, if we are going to be able cover our needs while working at editing full time, we need to ensure our per-hour rate matches our expenses and personal needs.

Some editors have less overhead than others. I'm not going to try and nitpick other editors' rates because that is both rude and unproductive. However, please recognize that, unless someone is trying to intentionally mislead you, they charge what they charge for a reason. Chances are, they have the education, skills, and knowledge to back that up, too.

How to Vet Your Editor

Since you're going to be hiring someone to work on your book and likely spend a great deal of money on this endeavor, you are going to want to vet this person before sending them a check. This can be done any number of ways, and no legitimate editor will be offended by you asking these questions. If someone is offended by your vetting process, then you should carefully consider if you want to work with them.

Obtain a sample edit

Most editors gladly provide sample edits to prospective clients at either no cost or a very low cost. As a general rule, a sample edit will be somewhere around 1,000 words (though this varies by editor) from somewhere in the middle of your book. Keep in mind that you cannot really provide sample edits for developmental editing as it is far too large scale to do in such a small way, but some editors have methods of giving you a rough idea.

The sample edit will show you the editor's style and feedback and provide you the opportunity to see what you think of them in action. You can then use this metric to decide if they are a good fit for you and your project. Also, sample edits allow the editor to gauge how much work is going to be needed for your manuscript and give them the ability to provide a more detailed estimate of how much it will cost to complete.

Review their website

While editors aren't professional web designers, as a rule, they should have solid websites that give you an idea of their services, who they are as people, any credentials they might possess, and provide testimonials from clients they have worked with in the past. In addition to that, they will likely have links to any public-facing social media, blogs, or other media they have. A wonderful example of an editing website that isn't mine is the one my friend Crystal Watanabe runs, Pikko's House. Another worthy example is Dick Margulis Creative Services.

My website is also indicative of what I do. My company is Insomnia Self-Publishing Services and is an example of another site that demonstrates work done.

Check professional organization affiliations

Not all professional editors of merit are members of a professional organization, so this is not a hard requirement. However, shysters who just want to bilk you for money rarely will be members of one because that costs money, and some of the organizations vet their members. Some do not, but the act of purchasing a membership is a step very few charlatans would actually take.

Some of the editing organizations you might see are: ACES, CIEP, EFA, SFEP, Editors Canada (EC), NAIWE, Society of Editors (Australia), Indian Copyeditors Forum (India), SWET (Japan), SENSE (Netherlands), and many more.

Ask around and see if you can find clients of theirs in writing groups.

Again, this may not turn much up for you if they aren't in the same circles as you, but it's worth a gamble to see if anybody has heard of them! If nobody has that you can find, that doesn't mean they aren't legitimate, but word of mouth carries weight. If you can find any, it may be worth checking out.

Review their social media, blogs, and articles.

Not all editors have active social media for their company and work, but many of us have at least some public-facing presence. Otherwise, how would we market? I have a weekly blog, a YouTube Channel, a TikTok channel, an Instagram page, and am across social media both as an editor and as an author, so I'm easy to find. Many editors do similar things.

Just be aware, you shouldn't friend them or stalk their personal page uninvited. We are allowed to have personal lives, and many editors keep a strict space between their personal and public lives. Don't take it personally if they decline a Facebook friend request.

Ask about their contract.

Most every professional editor I have ever met who is out of their first few years works with contracts. Our contracts protect both us and our clients and are usually straightforward. Many of them will look similar and may even be boilerplate since some editing organizations provide that as a service to editors with memberships. However, if they have a contract that provides adequate coverage for you and the editor, chances are they aren't a shark.

Identifying Scammers

If you've gone through the steps of vetting someone, you should have a good idea of whether or not the person is a scammer. There are, however, a few markers you should be conscious of that aren't on that list. Not all of these are immediately indicative of a scam on their face, but if you put them all together, you can build a clearer picture.

One of the first indicators of a scammer is them approaching you unsolicited, just like I've been howling about through this whole book. But after that, you can look for some specifics. One of the big ones is making big promises. If they promise your book will be an NYT Bestseller, or if they promise that there will be *no* errors and that your book will be *perfect* when they're done with it, chances are they aren't being honest.

No editor worth their red pen would ever make that promise to a client. In fact, most of us have in our contracts that working with us is not a guarantee of sales, publication, or anything else. We never guarantee "perfection" because what defines that is both ephemeral and unobtainable. If perfection were possible, you'd think we would never see a typo in a Stephen King book, and yet they exist.

The best we can guarantee is damn good.

Another indicator of questionable skills is if their website is rife with typos and errors. While editors are human, and I have caught my fair share of embarrassing typos on my own website (because I have sometimes been editing website copy at 3 a.m.), the website should be clean. It also shouldn't read like ChatGPT marketing copy.

Asking questions will also help you determine if this person knows what they're talking about or not. Ask them about the different types of editing, ask them about their experience in the industry, ask them what they think about the Oxford comma. If you can get them talking about writing and editing a little, it will be clear quickly if they can keep up with the conversation, even if it's just via email. You can also ask them what genres they have experience in.

Finally, we have the issue of price. While I won't say anyone charging extremely low rates is a scammer, if someone is charging rock-bottom rates without a solid explanation (they're new, it's a hobby, or they're retired and just keeping busy), then you need to give it some serious side eye. As I've shown in some of the previous chapters, editing isn't cheap if you want the good stuff. If someone is offering to do a line edit for $300 on your 90,000-word novel over the course of a weekend, they're definitely not the good stuff.

Summary

This chapter was a dense one where we discussed the process of finding, vetting, and hiring an editor. Your editor is oftentimes one of the closest people to your manuscript outside of yourself, and that means you absolutely must identify someone with whom you can have a good, healthy relationship built on trust.

Key Takeaways

- There are many types of editing out there as well as some things that fall under the umbrella but aren't strictly editing—like book coaching. Identifying the services you need and what order you need them in will help you find the right editor for you.

- Understanding that editing is an important service with a great deal of depth and nuance can both help you make sure you connect with the right editor for you as well as explain much of its value.

- Make sure you vet your editor(s) thoroughly and ask them questions before hiring them! There are many red flags that you are dealing with a scammer and not a real editor, and knowing how to identify those red flags can save you a lot of difficulty and money.

- Scammers are all over the place, and they are particularly pernicious when it comes to new authors. They often pop up on social media and will stalk writers' groups looking for new marks. Being careful in these environments is absolutely necessary to safeguarding your work and your wallet!

Chapter Nine

Typesetting Crash Course

Before we get too deep into this, I want to state clearly that this chapter is not a replacement for hiring a typesetter. I can give you some of the basic skills you'll want to deploy and get you started learning how to do it, but if you want a good-looking book, you'll want to either do further study on your own or hire someone else to do this for you.

The point of this is to give you a leg up on starting the journey, not replace working with someone who has walked the road a long time. Typesetting is an art form unto itself and takes practice, study, dedication, and an exacting nature.

Typesetting Introduction and Software

There are two distinct routes to take if you want to typeset and format your own books. One is cheaper and faster but provides you fewer options and less customization. One is more expensive and requires practice and study but gives you a vast array of customization and options.

As with so many elements of this process, there's no wrong answer here. Personally, I'm a snob and prefer the slower method of doing everything by hand at this point because the software that allows you to do it with a button press doesn't have enough customization for me, and I am cranky about that fact. I have, however, been doing typesetting for a decade now, so I am persnickety.

So, to break this into software by category, here are the two types:

Book Design Software

- Adobe InDesign
- Affinity Publisher
- Scribus
- Microsoft Publisher

Automated Software

- Atticus
- Vellum (Mac only)

Atticus and Vellum produce adequate-quality books, but both have limitations to customization. They are excellent for people who don't want to study typesetting and do it themselves. Typesetting, admittedly, is a specialized skill that requires a certain attention to detail and enjoyment of things like fonts. It definitely isn't something everyone will want to, or even necessarily be able to, get into.

You also need to be aware of fonts in a way you probably never have before. Like photography, words, and other mediums, fonts are actually somebody's intellectual property, and knowing what fonts you can and cannot use for what purposes is almost a hobby unto itself.

One of the selling points of Atticus and Vellum is that they have a small library of fonts you can choose from, which they guarantee you have the right to use for your designs. So, if you don't want to spend hours searching through font catalogs either downloading free-for-commercial use fonts, or purchase commercial licenses for fonts that aren't free, those two programs provide you with a base to work from.

I will note, however, that both Atticus and Vellum are geared more toward either fiction or non-fiction that is formatted like fiction. If you are writing a non-fiction work that requires text boxes, pull quotes, and a lot of internal formatting of that nature, you may find them inadequate for that task. Also, if your work is that complex to typeset, you may want to consider hiring a professional. Alternatively, you could practice with typesetting a book that is going to be simpler in layout and work up to your more complex manuscript.

As to the other typesetting software on the list, the one that everyone will have heard about is Adobe InDesign. It is considered the gold standard—or, frankly, *was*. At this point, Affinity software outstrips Adobe in my book. Plus, Affinity isn't a subscription model. If you purchase your software, you have a lifetime license for it, and the cost is extremely reasonable for the entire suite of programs (Affinity Photo, Affinity Publisher, and Affinity Designer). For those of you familiar with InDesign, you will find Affinity a worthy replacement should you decide you don't want to either pay an egregious amount of money or pay monthly for it.

The only other software I want to mention by name on this list is Scribus. It's clunky, the interface is outdated, and I don't really like using it. However, the thing it has going for it is the price tag: free. Scribus is open source software that will allow you to do typesetting if you don't have the money to invest into any of the above listed software at all. It's by far not the most comfortable to use on this list, but it is noteworthy as being accessible to those who may not have the capability to pay.

Basic Principles and Lexicon

At its heart, typesetting is the art of laying a book out so it looks good in print. Ebook formatting is referred to as "formatting" rather than typesetting since the term "typesetting" comes from the art of placing type into the printing press frames by hand. As an aside anecdote, the terms "upper case" and "lower case" refer to which side of the carrying case the letters came from. The "lower case" was easier to access and used more frequently since there are usually fewer upper case letters in most printed works.

There, that's a thing you know now. You're welcome. I dub thee an honorary typesetting nerd.

Beyond that, there are some terms you need to know in reference to typesetting before we get too far into things.

- Widows are lines of text that are the start of a paragraph alone on a page by themselves.

- Orphans are lines of text or a singular word at the end of a paragraph that run onto the next page.

- Leading refers to the strips of lead historical typesetters used to space lines of text, and thusly, in the modern day, it refers to the space between lines.

- Kerning refers to the space between individual letters.

- Styles refer to specific attributes of text or paragraphs (such as font, size, color, placement, formatting, etc.) within your software.

If you are using the software that automatically typesets your book for you, you won't need to worry much about any of these things except "styles." Styles is how they will refer to things like your chapter headings and whether or not you use a dropcap, that big letter at the start of a segment.

Now that we have the lexicon out of the way, let's talk some of the foundations. First is that I have a video tutorial of all of this on YouTube that shows you how to typeset in Affinity Publisher. I strongly suggest giving it a watch because typesetting is all about visuals, and without them, it's hard to explain a lot of the process.

It is time for me to bestow upon you one of the most important pieces of knowledge I can impart. This is a piece of wisdom that keeps typesetters up at night, and it makes us break into cold sweat whenever someone suggests it: *Do not typeset your manuscript in word processing software.* Seriously. You can make something look book-ish in it, but it won't hold a candle to what you can do with proper software, and word processing software was never designed to typeset documents. You can format *ebooks* in word processing software for the most part, but never, ever should you use it for print. To do so angers some ancient eldritch horror.

Okay, fine, the ancient eldritch horror here is me, but let's not quibble over details.

My bellowing aside, the process of typesetting doesn't start in your typesetting software. It actually *does* begin in your word processing software. The process, however, does not end there. For this, you will absolutely need software that has text styles, which means Word, Scrivener (which does some), Libre Office, or any other writing software that uses text styles. I lament that yWriter does not, but since I use Word to do my final editing and preparations for typesetting anyway, I can soothe my wounded soul with that.

In addition to understanding the lexicon, there are also a few basic principles of typesetting with which you should be familiar before we start.

Font choice is an art form.

Choosing the correct fonts for a project is truly its own art form that comes with its own rules. There are a few I am going to go over in the next segment, but understanding that this is of extreme importance is something I'm going to talk about a few times in this chapter. Best to introduce it early.

Accessibility is not a buzzword.

When we are talking typesetting, we want our books to be accessible. This means considering dyslexia, people who have issues with eyesight or blindness, and other such accommodations. I'm not going to lay out every possible thing you need to know here, but the more accessible your book is (multiple formats, few or no embedded fonts, etc.), the better off you will be. It doesn't require a great deal of money to make your print and ebooks accessible if you cannot do audio books off the bat. Screen readers will allow people to access them just fine if you format them well and use alt text!

The small details really matter.

Things like making sure you don't have an indent at the start of a chapter or scene, making sure you don't have widows and orphans, and turning off auto-hyphenation are things that make a massive difference in the visuals of a book. Readers might not know why they really gravitate toward a professionally typeset or formatted book, but they unerringly do.

Typesetting and formatting are not an afterthought.

As with the previous statement, how your book looks on the page should not be tertiary. It really makes more of an impact than you might know. Most readers don't study formatted books to death like us typesetters do, but they will unconsciously become aware of things they cannot explain. Quality formatting and typesetting might not save an awful manuscript, but bad typesetting can do a lot to damage a reader's experience with a good manuscript.

Font Choices

There are entire books written on typography that I'm not going to try and duplicate here. Typography is an entire art form unto itself, and trying to condense something like *The Elements of Typographic Style* into one sub-section of a single chapter would both not do it justice and mean this subsection would be the size of the rest of the book.

Instead of trying to explain *everything* about font choice, I'm going to break this down into a few ideas you can take forward and use to begin your journey into studying typography if that's something you might find interesting to explore. If not, it'll give you enough to do some typesetting of your own books without sticking your foot in it.

The last broad-strokes thing I'm going to address before we get into specifics is that ebooks and print books are very different beasties. Ebooks are not in a fixed format, meaning they will change depending on what device they are being viewed on, and readers have the choice of changing fonts, font sizes, and more. This is an accessibility tool and should not be fought against. It does, however, mean you have dramatically less control over ebooks than you do print when it comes to certain things, so you need to consider that.

What You Need to Know

The first thing I want to bring up is that not all fonts are created equal. And no, I'm not here to dunk on Comic Sans. What I mean by this is, fonts have jobs to do. Body fonts, like this one you're reading now, are different from heading fonts, like the chapter title and the name of this sub-section, which are different yet again from decorative fonts, like what you might see on a greeting card. They all have different purposes. Using the wrong font for the wrong job is a recipe for disaster just as surely as mixing up salt and sugar in a baking recipe. Some fonts are also objectively terrible (illegible, unattractive, not good at their job).

No, Comic Sans is not one of them. It might have been dramatically overused to the point of achieving meme status, but it is an excellent font to draft in and wonderful for readability for certain groups of people. I don't advise using it for professional products, but as a font to draft your novel in? It actually is a good option for a number of reasons, including encouraging a certain playfulness and lack of rigidity that helps the creative process.

What Fonts to Choose and How to Choose Them

For typesetting and ebook formatting purposes, you have two primary categories of fonts to think of. Some books get complex in the fonts department (such as *Ready Player One*), but in general, you will only need two primary categories: heading fonts and body fonts. Decorative fonts serve very little purpose in print typesetting because they are often not extremely legible (think handwritten signatures, for example). They are also often inappropriate for most genres of books. Let's leave them to greeting cards, graphic design, and maybe some book cover elements here and there.

The last piece of information I am going to give you before digging in is a definition. You have likely seen "serif" and "sans serif" or just "sans" thrown around before. Serif fonts are the ones that have little lines at the top and bottom of letters, such as on the ends of the line of the "S" in Times New Roman or Georgia. Sans serif fonts do not have that extra line with some examples of this being Arial, Comic Sans, and Calibri.

Heading Fonts

Heading fonts are your chapter and section headers. For fiction, you won't see much for heading fonts outside the chapter headers unless you have some smaller formatting indicating a change of place or time. Those are also considered headings rather than body text. Heading styles come in layers, usually labelled Heading 1 (H1) down through Heading 4 (H4). You can have more than that, but if you need more than three or four heading layers, there's a chance you're writing a business document and/or have just gotten a little over-excited.

Font-wise, Heading 1 is going to be your chapter header font. You can have it be as decorative or plain as you choose, but if you are going to go with decorative, I suggest looking at fonts popular in your genre. Romance fonts tend to be swooshy, swoopy fonts, whereas thriller fonts are often sharp-edged and a little menacing. Science fiction tends toward sans-serif fonts that have more verticality. Fantasy often likes either plain typeface or more Medieval-flavored fonts. Non-fiction is all over the place, from swooshy fonts for books aimed at religious women, to high-impact, high-visibility fonts for self-help to make you feel a sense of urgency.

No matter what font you choose for your headings, make sure it is *easily readable*. This means no matter how pretty the font is, you need to type the words "Chapter 1" or "Chapter One" in it to see how it's going to look. If you can't read it immediately and clearly, skip it and try another. While heading fonts definitely should be "cool," they also help readers know where they are in a book. If readers can't read them easily, then the headings aren't doing their job.

Some excellent heading fonts are Garamond, Open Sans, Gotham, Hoefler, Trade Gothic, Bodoni, Helvitica, Caslon, Baskerville, and Sabon.

Body Fonts

Body fonts are the bulk of your text and have some nuance to them. You want a font that conveys the feel of the book while also being easy to read and absorb. They need to be open and wide enough to breathe on the page without taking up so much space that they increase your page count by too much. On average, the print book market considers a "page" to be approximately 250 words. This means your body font should get you about to that place. In books with a larger trim size (6 x 9 etc.), you are likely to have more words per page, so you don't need to make your font size 24 pt to conform to that.

As a rule, you want your body font to be no smaller than 11 pt. This is a little flexible because some fonts are bigger than others by design, but 11 pt is the average with the range being between 10 pt and 12 pt, depending on the font itself. You also are shooting for something where the letters are wide enough that they aren't jammed together, which hurts readability and causes eye strain. If you are doing a large print book, you will want to consider doing a font size of around 14 pt for your body text.

For print books, you want to lean toward serif fonts (serif is easier to read than sans-serif in print as a rule), whereas for ebooks, you should lean toward sans-serif fonts with the understanding that readers can change the font themselves in their reading apps.

Much the same as with heading fonts, body fonts have different feels to them for different genres, so you should take a look around and see what's out there in your genre. However, some of the old standby fonts for body text are Garamond, Times New Roman, Georgia, Cambria, Baskerville, Caslon, and Sabon. Personally, I like Georgia and Cambria, but that's just a function of taste. I also find Times New Roman a little narrow for my eyes (I'm dyslexic) and favor more open fonts. Garamond is considered one of the most readable fonts on the market by many people and is an excellent choice.

Interior Design

When we're talking "interior design" here, we don't mean your curtains, your rug, or your furniture. I'm not judging yours; you don't judge mine. My house looks like thrift store meets Dollar Tree chic. What I'm talking about here are design elements like graphics, text boxes, margins, page numbers, and so on.

Much as with typography, these elements will vary by genre and by personal taste. Some authors like having chapter heading art, whereas others would rather burn their book than insert it. There's no wrong answer here. There are, however, some considerations.

The first is that all images put in your print book (again, ebooks are a different beastie) should be 300 dpi (dots per inch). Anything under 300 dpi will not have good fidelity at the printer, and anything too much over that will lose detail because the printers can only cram so much ink into a space.

The second consideration is that your images will be black and white unless you want to spend a lot of money on printing. Color printing is *not* cheap and best left to art books, photo books, or other such endeavors. If you're printing anything where words are the primary focus, you're best off embracing the grayscale unless you really want to spend an egregious amount of money per book. You're allowed to make that mistake.

In general, fiction will require minimal design elements outside of your chapter heading elements, maybe a unique scene break image, and doing some kind of special drop cap if you have a book, or an edition of a book, where inserting one would be a benefit. Illuminated—as in manuscript illuminations, not as in light—drop caps in special editions of fantasy books are a big hit.

Another interior design element you might consider for certain genres is a map. Fantasy readers love maps and have deep affection for them in books where geography and travel times are of importance. Tolkien had his beautiful map in *The Lord of the Rings*, Raymond E. Feist had Midkemia in his *Riftwar* books, and Garth Nix has an excellent map for his *Old Kingdom* series.

For non-fiction, you'll want to consider things like charts, graphs, text boxes, and quotes. In ebooks, you can only do so much due to the limitations of the format, so I'd leave fancy elements out unless they're necessary, like a chart or graph. In print, you can use the space to full effect to create a far more interesting visual. Textbooks also regularly use images to help give a break from large swaths of text and provide context and depth.

When considering interior design elements, I do want to caution against doing things that will be "too much." You don't want to distract from or crowd the words, so I advise against over-embellishing your book with interior design and attempting to guild the lily. You are better off using them to poignant effect, but not to excess. I also strongly recommend working with a professional graphic designer to do these layout elements since their expertise will help ensure your book looks the way you hope it will.

Ebook vs. Print

As I mentioned a few times throughout this segment, ebook and print are entirely different creatures. Print books are, by their nature, a "fixed format." This means the elements on the page don't move. In digital formats, a PDF is considered a "fixed format" as well. If you zoom in on one, you need to scroll rather than having everything resized for you. Ebooks, on the other hand, are dynamic formats. They will resize themselves and change their text flow based on what device is viewing them, what the screen size is, and allow readers to change fonts and so on for accessibility reasons.

With ebooks, less is more almost all the time. You can do what's called "embed fonts" into ebook files, which means your heading or other fonts will look *exactly* the same no matter what you do absent changing the size for accessibility reasons, but some apps and devices don't take kindly to that and break when you do it. Some file formats also don't like it as much and are finicky. As such, I advise against embedding fonts unless it is something extremely important to the book itself.

The only circumstance where I embedded all the fonts was a novel where there were multiple different types of communication (it was a LitRPG novel) that had different fonts and different quotation marks. Some used < > while others used " " or ' ' and so on. It was a complex book that needed the fonts for clarity's sake. Other than that, I sometimes will embed heading fonts if I'm feeling particularly sticky about it, but I try to avoid doing that too much because of the reasons above.

Another thing to know about ebooks is that, unlike print books, you do not format them in Affinity Publisher or Adobe InDesign. You can use Atticus or Vellum to produce them or, if you don't want to use them, you can do most of the work in good ol' Word or Libre Office, and then use a free conversion software called "Calibre" to export them into your ebook file type of choice. At the time of writing, .epub reigns supreme, but other notables include .mobi, which is technically discontinued by Amazon, and .azw3, Amazon's new native format. In general, though, all distribution platforms with which I am familiar accept .epub files.

Choosing whether to put your book into print or not is a decision you'll want to make based on your market and your wallet. Wrap-around covers are more expensive than an ebook cover for obvious reasons, typesetting by a professional is not cheap, and printing them means overhead. On the upside, physical copies of your books are an excellent way to sell at events, do signings at bookstores, and sell on your own website if you want to do signed copies that way. Brick-and-mortar bookstores also will only deal in print copies, so if that is part of your sales model, you'll want to keep that in mind.

Some authors release books in ebook first, then use the sales to put money into paperback versions. That is also a valid strategy. You don't need to start with both if you don't have the ability to do so. Some genres also do well enough in ebook that you might not even want to bother with a paperback version unless bookstores are your target market and you want print copies in local libraries.

Why Not Word?

This is a question I hear all the time, and I have gotten push back from authors on this point. While I recognize that learning *yet another* skill and having *yet another* program can be frustrating, there are good reasons for it. None of them are elitist garbage, either.

Also, there *are* people who can make passable print books with Word. I've met them. I know it's possible, but the folks doing it were computer engineers who cajoled Word into doing things it wasn't entirely meant to do. Also, Word is pushing to try and do some of the things other programs do, like facing pages. However, it's still lacking a few elements that are extremely useful and sometimes of vital importance, like master pages.

And let's not even talk about how much of a pain it can be with images. Move an image from one point to another direction, and sirens go off in the distance, missiles launch, and the world ends.

Typesetting for print in Word is like using the wrong knife in the kitchen. Sure, you can probably make a delicious meal using just a steak knife, but you'll work faster, more efficiently, and have a better time of it if you use the proper knife for the job.

While Word has begun to allow you to do things like manually adjusting leading and kerning and facing pages (which is a new addition with the recent iteration, I believe), it isn't set up to make that process easy. We're back to the knife in the kitchen. Sure, you *can* peel a pound of potatoes with a steak knife, but you'll do it faster and better with a peeler or even a paring knife.

The tools Word has for things like that kind of work are usually buried under a few layers of menus, making them inconvenient to access. As such, you need to take several extra steps to accomplish what you're trying to do rather than having access to the tools in dramatically more convenient and customizable places.

I also want to note that the vast majority of people looking to typeset their own books and who think they can squeak by with Word are folks who haven't studied typesetting and may not realize what they're doing or why. The vast majority of folks who do things like that commit cardinal sins of typesetting, such as having a paragraph indent at the start of a chapter. While that's not a function of the software they're using, it's usually an indicator that the book wasn't structured by a professional.

In fact, I would make the argument that, just like a professional chef *could* work with nothing but a steak knife, they just plain wouldn't *want* to. Something having the capacity to jury-rig it into obeying is one discussion, but the other is more about whether it's worth doing. Right now, Affinity Publisher 2 is available for purchase for $69.99 (nice). Their entire suite of programs is $164.99. A subscription to Word is $99.99/year. So for the price of less than one year of Microsoft 365 for personal use, you could own typesetting software.

I fully recognize that some people may not have the financial ability to purchase software right now and might be considering trying to typeset in Libre Office, which has even fewer options than Word. If you are one of those people, look into Scribus. It, like Libre Office (an open source, free software), is not as pleasant to work in or quite as powerful as its for-pay counterparts, but it'll get the job done and give you the tools you need.

Scribus is never my first suggestion, but if it's that or Libre Office, I'll recommend Scribus every time.

Summary

Typesetting is an under-appreciated art form by many people in the publishing industry. New authors often skip this step entirely and end up hurting their own book sales by doing so. While it's always best to hire a professional to do these tasks, you can learn typesetting on your own if you want to take the time to do so. That said, neglecting it entirely is a terrible plan. However you go about the process of typesetting your book, it is an entirely necessary step on the road to publishing.

Key Takeaways

- Choosing the correct software to typeset in is an important step in the process of your book. Using the wrong software will result in excess frustration, a poor quality end product, and much crying and gnashing of teeth.

- Since it is its own art form, typesetting has its own language and also has many nuances to enhance accessibility for readers. Knowing how to make your books readable to a larger audience will not only earn you more sales but also show you as an author care about your readers.

- Font choices are extremely important and knowing what fonts to use and where is a science unto itself. Doing research into fonts and font choices is a necessity if you are intending to typeset books on your own.

- Typesetting for print is different than typesetting for ebooks. Ebooks have a different format and must be simplistic due to them being read on multiple devices unless you are doing a fixed format ebook (.pdf-only). Understanding this difference is vital if you are producing your own books.

- Please, don't use word processing programs to typeset in. Some people do it successfully, but they are an extreme rarity, and I really, really don't recommend it for anyone if you can avoid it.

Chapter Ten

Distribution Decisions

One of the final choices for your book before it's out for sale is choosing your distribution method. This will be your means of getting it out into the world and in front of your audience. It's one of those things that people tend to balk at when they're encountering it for the first time because it feels huge. There are so many printers out there and so many bookstores that it feels like an incredibly overwhelming decision.

Fortunately, it isn't. There aren't as many decisions as you might think, and there are several services available that will allow you to distribute to large swaths of the population of the world by uploading to one of them. You don't need to panic.

There are, however, a few key choices about distribution you'll need to make that we're going to address in this chapter. It isn't as massive a field as it seems at first, and you'll find that choosing distribution methods will be less daunting than you think by the time we're done.

One of the first parts of this process is identifying your genre. You might think you know what it is or that it doesn't matter very much, but let's walk through the steps anyway. Genre is of extreme importance, and ensuring you are in the right one(s) will make or break your sales on a lot of platforms.

Identifying your genre is another of those decisions that feels more complicated than it is a lot of the time. Many authors also go about it with the wrong thought process, which leads to problems not only for them but for other authors. Being careless with their genres pollutes the pool and confuses people.

I also want to stab one specific piece of really bad advice in the neck before we go any further: *Do not find a random subcategory to stick your book into in order to be at the top of it.* This advice has floated around for a while, and since genres are not well-policed on certain platforms, people sometimes fly under the radar while shelving bigfoot erotica in some tiny, obscure non-fiction category that nobody knows exists. By sales alone, it often rises to the top of that category, and then these people claim they're bestsellers.

Don't be those people.

Not only is it extremely dishonest, it also doesn't work well, and it will only create problems for you and your readers. Beyond that, anybody can claim that their book is a bestseller without proof to back it up, so claiming bestseller status isn't a ticket to success these days. Trying to game the system will only result in misery, disdain from your peers, and consternation by readers.

Now that I've wrestled that particular demon, let's get on to discussing how you *actually* handle genre.

With books, you will have *two* genres (BISAC codes) you can enter your book into with most listings. Bowker gives you two, Ingram Spark gives you two, Draft2Digital gives you two, and Amazon gives you three. For reference, a BISAC code means "Book Industry Standards and Communications." It is the largest accepted system of categorization used by bookstores and libraries all over the world. It is used by publishers, librarians, and bookstores to shelve books and is extremely important for those individuals. Amazon uses "categories" rather than BISAC codes, but most Amazon categories are, in fact, the BISAC categories.

They are sorted through a system of subcategories that is usually referenced like this: Fiction > Romance >

Fantasy, where "Fiction" is the broad category, "Romance" is the primary genre, and "Fantasy" is the subgenre. If you want to get technical, Fiction > Romance > Fantasy is FIC027030, fic being "Fiction." 027 is for "romance," and "030" is for "fantasy." The BISG (Book Industry Study Group) has a comprehensive list of BISAC codes on their website that you can peruse, and you will probably never need to know the numeric code end of things unless you are going to become a librarian, bookseller, or publisher.

You don't have enough room there to force in every theoretical category you could possibly assign to your book, so rather than trying to do that, we need to drill down into the essence of the story. Think about the two things your story would collapse without in broad terms. Since I have been on a *Star Wars* kick while writing this (I blame watching the new season of *The Mandalorian*), I'm going to use *Episode IV* as an example yet again.

Watching it, we can see that the space and futuristic elements are extremely important to the setting. Removing those would leave us with a story that wouldn't make a great deal of sense. Without space travel, the rest of the story couldn't happen as it's written. So, we can see science fiction being one of the genre markers.

Next, we have the story itself. It is a classic adventure story complete with the Hero's Journey.

These two things together mean that the first BISAC I'd assign this would be Fiction > Science Fiction > Action & Adventure (FIC028010). That's pretty straightforward.

With our first BISAC category identified, I am going to look at others. Rather than straying too far, I think *Star Wars* is exclusively going to work as science fiction because you can't remove that element and have the story make sense. It's definitely not literary fiction. Not fantasy. Not romance, despite having some romantic elements in the series. Romantic elements does not a romance make.

Instead, I am going to place it squarely into Space Opera. It fulfills those genre requirements and, in fact, is considered one of the essential works in the genre. So, our second BISAC is Fiction > Science Fiction > Space Opera (FIC028030).

In Amazon, you have the ability to add one more genre, so let's pretend we are doing so. While Amazon's categories are a little different than the BISAC ones, they're close enough that I don't really see a need to dig into Amazon for this exercise, so I'm sticking with the BISAC list for the purposes of this.

Skimming through, I don't see another category leap out at me. "Alien contact" doesn't really work because aliens are an intrinsic part of society, so it doesn't fit that criterion. Nor is it cyberpunk, military, romance, or space exploration. Rather than sticking in just subgenres of science fiction, if I back up a little and take a look around, I could make a pretty simple argument for putting it into action and adventure. So, I would pop it in there at the top level: Fiction > Action & Adventure (FIC002000). I could also go with top level science fiction instead if I chose, but in this case, I wanted to clearly illustrate you don't need to stick to a single category if you feel it straddles them.

Now, remember that howling I did about not putting your book in random subcategories? That still applies. However, you should try and find the narrowest categories your book qualifies for. Some categories are bigger than others, and some have a lot of weird issues from time to time with things getting polluted by fads. For example, as I write this, the genre I write in as a fiction author, urban fantasy, is currently swimming in paranormal romance and supernatural romance. I have recently re-categorized my books to avoid that because I keep getting shelved in with very spicy novels that are entirely unrelated to what I write (thrillers). I was shooting for comparable titles such as the *Dresden Files* and the *Iron Druid Chronicles*. But here we are.

That leads us to why this is so important.

Your genre will define where you are shelved and what books are your comparative works, according to the bookstore or algorithm. If your book doesn't fit next to other books in that genre on a shelf without clashing terribly, you have a problem.

There's also some bizarre tendency by some authors to become angry about certain genres. I have seen arguments where people yell that romances shouldn't *require* a "happily ever after" or "happily for now" to be romances. While you can make that argument if you want to, the reality is that genre is a *business* decision, not a referendum on your writing. Something can be incredibly romantic and not be a romance. And just because one or two of the really big names in the genre breaks with tradition doesn't mean you probably should buck the system.

The reason I say this is because readers use genre as a way to know what to expect. If they pick up a science fiction novel, they expect space and lasers and aliens, or at the very least, cyber enhancements and high technology. Thwarting that expectation entirely is not a good plan if you want to retain readers. Readers want to know what they're getting to a certain extent, just like me going to the store and buying cola. If I bought Coke and discovered it was Pepsi instead, I'd be furious. It doesn't matter that they're both colas; it wasn't what I was looking for or expecting. Genre is the same way.

Genre is just a marketing tool used to alert readers what to expect in your book. It gives them expectations of certain tropes, settings, and beats. You can certainly play with those expectations a little and subvert them to delight and surprise your readers. That said, you cannot mess up the core tenants of the genre entirely without severe blowback from the community. Angering your target readers is an excellent way to make absolutely no money selling your book.

I know some people wax on about "artistic integrity," but this isn't the place for that. Artistic integrity is important and valuable, but that's more about what you wrote. How you sell it is entirely divorced from that notion, and selling something as an urban fantasy or a supernatural thriller doesn't change the quality of the writing, characters, or story. It just tells readers what they're in for and helps you connect with the people who want to read your work.

Keywords and Why They Matter

I want to be the first person to tell you that I am not a keyword expert. I can explain the theory to you, but putting it into practice is an area of extreme difficulty for me. That said, I would be remiss if I didn't at least mention them and their importance when discussing distribution because all the retailers you upload to will ask about keywords.

In essence, keywords are a collection of words and short phrases that the search engine uses to drive traffic to your book. It will see those and send folks searching for similar things to your page. While the algorithm takes into consideration the back text of your book as well, keywords are going to be your most potent tool for telling the computer who to show your work to in their searches.

Keywords are *not* customer-facing for distributors. This means your customers won't see them listed on your page anywhere on Amazon or any other retailer. They are purely an internal means to have your book placed in their search function. The reason I say this is they're not meant to be marketing copy to lure people to your book or explain everything about it. They're just a handful of search terms that will guide people to your work.

Another thing to note is that book keywords are *different* than other types of marketing keywords. Picking up a course on how to market widgets on Amazon will give you some principles, but it won't teach you how to do it for *books* specifically. As with most things literary-related, books are their own thing entirely.

Whether it's my autism or some personal block, I really struggle with keywords at the point of writing this. I have severe problems thinking of what people would search for, but some of the useful keyword types I have been told about are things like specific tropes your book has (enemies to lovers, for example), things a shopper might specifically search for if they were looking for books like yours, and keywords where competition isn't too high.

I use Publisher Rocket to help me do keyword research. It is software developed by Kindlepreneur to help authors identify keywords and genres that aren't oversaturated and will yield the best bang for your buck. Rather than agonize over trying to teach you keywords myself, I am just going to suggest you visit Dave Chesson's website "Kindlepreneur.com" and do some reading there. He lays things out far better and in far more detail than I ever could.

Your Backmatter

When we think frontmatter, we think about the copyright page, a table of contents, and a dedication or acknowledgments. Sometimes, you'll have an introduction like in a non-fiction work, but it's mostly those things. Backmatter is rarely talked about, but it's just as important.

Backmatter is the space in the book after your story ends. How you leverage this space is going to have a significant impact on your sales. It can include things like a call to readers to join your newsletter or an advertisement for the next book in your series, or suggesting other reads from you if you aren't writing in a series. It's extremely valuable because the reader has just finished a book you have written and is primed to make another purchase or to keep up with you. It's a space you don't want to ignore.

There are a few schools of thought on whether you should do a newsletter sign-up or if you should just link to your next book in the series. Alternatively, ask them to leave you a review—though there's discussion to be had about whether you should ask this or allow their reading software to prompt them to do it. There's a lot of nuance to this that will depend on where you are in your writing career. You can also go back and update your backmatter in previous books, too, assuming you have the tools and know-how to do so.

Again, rather than try and claim to be an expert on this myself, I'm going to give you some broad strokes and then tell you go talk to Quinn Ward, who is a highly successful author and speaker. He does talks on this subject that provide incredible information, and his coaching work is over at "Write Your Own Path" (WriteYourOwnPath.com). You can also find numerous books on the specifics of this.

To KU or Not to KU

Ah, the question. KU stands for "Kindle Unlimited," which at this point is Amazon's exclusive distribution plan. If your ebook is in KU, it *explicitly* may not be available anywhere else. You may sell *print* books through other mediums, but you may not sell ebooks anywhere but on Amazon for the duration of your time in the Kindle Unlimited program (a.k.a. KDP Select). The default run is 90 days.

Rather than give you a hard and fast ruling on this, I'm going to give you information so you can make the decision on your own. Also, if you hear the term "going wide," that means publishing to other platforms beyond Amazon. These other platforms can include Kobo, Smashwords, Barnes and Noble, and other such distributors of ebooks.

It may seem simpler to just put your book into KU and forget it. Uploading to multiple distributors can seem like a pain and be overwhelming. It doesn't have to be, but many people see the options, freeze, and slink into KU because it seems like the safe option. I'm not saying you can't find success that way, but as with all business decisions, it's wiser to make an informed choice.

Let's start by exploring what KDP Select is in case you don't know how it works.

KDP Select is an Amazon program that provides content to the subscription service "Kindle Unlimited." Kindle Unlimited is the name of the subscription program as marketed to buyers. KDP Select is how you get there as an author.

The way it works is you provide your book to Amazon with the guarantee that your ebook will not be available on any other retailer during the terms of the KDP Select enrollment. This includes not giving your book away for free with the exception of ARC copies provided prior to publication.

In return, your book is available to Kindle Unlimited users. For every page read, you get paid a small royalty called the KENP rate. This rate fluctuates up and down based on the number of people in the program and the number of readers subscribed to Kindle Unlimited. Further, you will have access to certain kinds of promotions only authors in KDP Select can run, such as doing a free book promotion.

On the other hand, this exclusivity can be a problem for some authors. First off, Kindle is not the dominant app worldwide, so if your market is not the United States, you may suffer for this. Also, there have been situations where authors have been punished due to their book being pirated and uploaded for illegal distribution without their consent. Amazon's algorithm doesn't care whether your book is for sale on Barnes and Noble or if it was pirated. If they find it anywhere on the internet—and they *will* check, regularly—you'll be booted out of the system. That said, I know if you contact Amazon support, they will usually show grace to someone who has had their books pirated versus someone willfully breaking terms and conditions.

It also limits your marketing versatility in certain ways that I won't get too deep into. Suffice to say, you can't do permafree books if you're in KDP select. Permafree, however, is less used these days as a tactic to get people into a series, so it's becoming less and less of an issue over time.

Some genres do *really* well in Kindle Unlimited (e.g., romance in particular, and thrillers like the *Jack Reacher* series). Others really don't do quite as well, and if you don't have a series to encourage read through, you aren't going to necessarily get as big a slice of the pie. It can be worth it for some people, but you'll need to do your own evaluations.

Here's where we start getting into my opinions. These are based on my experience and personal values and are not to be considered unbiased factual points.

Personally, I find KU odious. The idea of giving one retailer that much of the pie bothers me on a fundamental level. It just helps the megacorporation grow mega-er (it's a word now, shut up) by giving them all the content. I won't pretend Amazon isn't the biggest retailer in the world when it comes to books. They are absolutely the frontrunner, but they are far from the only horse in the race.

Other retailers may not have the same slice of the pie that Amazon does, but if you write in a genre that doesn't do uniquely well in KU, you aren't losing out by going wide. In fact, you'll be gaining access to markets that would otherwise be unavailable. Not to mention the ability to sell your book on your personal author website and make 100% of the sale price rather than closer to 40%.

There's also the "all eggs in one basket" mentality at work here. If Amazon exploded tomorrow, and all the servers went dark and you had your book available nowhere but Amazon then you'd have no readers on other platforms. You'd have to upload it there anyway in order to keep existing. Going wide means you can access other distributors, and if something happens to one of them? Well, you still have everybody else.

Then there are things like BookBub deals, which are a huge and sought-after marketing avenue. If you are not in KU, BookBub is more likely to accept your pitch because they serve readers on multiple platforms.

Amazon desperately wants to be the only player in the game. That's hardly a secret to anybody. Giant companies like that are like the creature No Face from *Spirited Away*. They grow larger and more problematic with every smaller company they consume and offer rewards for making deals with them that will only lead to you being consumed as well.

I know this sounds bitter, and it is a little, but the bitterness is more on principle than anything. I distribute books through Amazon, too. Heck, you might be reading this on your Kindle app right now. I'm not suggesting you eschew Amazon as the biggest market you can get into, but making it your *only* market is, in my mind, not the best choice for the world as a whole.

Doing a KU run once in a while just like you'd run a sale isn't a terrible option, to be clear. But most authors don't do things that way because removing your book from distribution everywhere else for nine months and then bringing it back is a recipe for frustration if you've built up a fan base on other sites.

The choice is ultimately yours, and I recognize and respect that. I don't think less of authors who are in KU because for some people, it's just plain the best market to be in. I'm not going to cast shade on those doing their best. But for me? No, thanks.

Distribution Options

This is where the rubber meets the road.

Currently, there are three major distribution options available to authors for both print and ebook options: IngramSpark, Draft2Digital (D2D), and KDP (Amazon). They are not mutually exclusive, and they all come with different plusses and minuses. Audiobook platforms are many, and things are shifting in that sphere. I am not an expert on audiobooks and hesitate to venture an opinion on it, but I do want to give it a mention since it *is* a thing.

Before we get into the discussion of whether Ingram or D2D is better, let's start with the fact that, no matter which of the above you choose, I strongly suggest uploading your book to Amazon separately. Uploading to Amazon (whether ebook or print) will ensure it is both never out of stock and allow you access to Amazon ads, which you will not have if you enable distribution for ebooks to Amazon via other distributors. KDP's printing is good quality, though they are finicky and weird about their cover dimensions at times in ways other distributors aren't. That's something your cover designer can help you with, so don't worry too much.

Of the three above distributors, only two will get your book into libraries and brick-and-mortar bookstores: IngramSpark and Draft2Digital. Both of these distributors are large, trustworthy, and have many options. At the time of writing, Draft2Digital has fewer print options than IngramSpark for hardcover books or children's book formats. They are, however, expanding options all the time, so it's entirely possible that when you read this, that will have changed.

Both IngramSpark and Draft2Digital offer print and ebook distribution to all major retailers. Both IngramSpark and Draft2Digital offer quality print books at comparable prices for printing and shipping. Both IngramSpark and Draft2Digital offer library and brick-and-mortar bookstore ordering. There are a few differences between them, but not very many, and some of the things that are different between them may well be in flux, so I don't want to dig too deeply into the current details. It is worth noting that, in fact, Draft2Digital uses Ingram's printing and distribution power to get physical books to retailers.

The major difference I have noticed is that, since 2020, IngramSpark has not had particularly good response times and has had a habit of having orders arrive late without explanation. Prior to that, they were quick to reply and had very reasonable shipping times, so this may be a temporary bump in the road, but I can say that it's been a three-year bump. As a result, I migrated over to Draft2Digital.

Also, until very recently, IngramSpark had an expensive upload fee with no revisions after upload unless you paid for them. Draft2Digital had no upload fee and revisions available at set intervals to allow for their internals to catch up. This has, however, changed. IngramSpark has now waived their upload fee and allows revisions up to a certain time after publication with no charge, though that time is finite.

Either of these options will, however, serve you perfectly well, and if you pair them with uploading your book to KDP directly, you should run into few issues.

Finally, I do want to note that it technically means you get less money if you allow D2D or IngramSpark to handle distribution to other sellers like Kobo or Barnes and Noble. If you upload to them all directly, you make the highest profit margin. However, what you lose is convenience. You also end up with very complex bank statements that make tracking your book sales for taxes a nightmare if you aren't the kind of person who handles those well.

Personally, I use a combination of Draft2Digital and Amazon KDP at this time. I have used IngramSpark in the past, and if they figure out their communication and shipping times, I could be lured back. This decision comes down to figuring out where things are at any current time and what you need out of a distributor.

Also, at the time of writing this, I want to note that Draft2Digital's ebook distribution is superior to IngramSpark's in terms of user friendliness and reach. At least in my opinion.

Summary

Deciding on where to distribute your book and how to go about getting it there is a more significant decision than many authors give credence to. The choice to go wide or be Amazon-exclusive is something you will want to do some deep thinking about as you move forward in your career. Also, understanding things like keywords, BISAC categories, and so on will help you ensure your book reaches your target audience.

Key Takeaways

- Using the correct keywords will help your audience locate your book on various platforms. Keywords are an extremely important part of your distribution process, no matter what platform(s) you choose to distribute to.

- The backmatter of your book is important and valuable to both selling future books and providing readers the opportunity to connect with you, the author. Using that space effectively can make a big difference to your book sales.

- Kindle Unlimited is a tool available to authors, but it has benefits and drawbacks both. Some genres and individuals swear by it and have found great success there. Other people have found far less success using that tool and do better publishing wide.

- For those going wide, choosing a distributor will have an impact on your bottom line as well as which markets you have access to. Some distributors are also more user-friendly than others. Trying things out for yourself and doing research will help you make effective decisions for yourself and your books.

Chapter Eleven

Marketing Principles

We are now reaching the part of the book I'm sure most of you have been either dreading or wanting to read most. Marketing your book(s) is one of those things that takes a long time and a lot of work that drags us kicking and screaming out of our comfort zone.

Writers and creatives typically aren't the most social creatures. We frequently prefer to be hidden away in our writing caves, hissing at intruders and drinking caffeinated beverages. Despite being cave gremlins, success in writing requires us to be prepared to leave our comfort zone and at least fake being human once in a while. Or at the very least stop biting people.

All joking aside, coming out of our shells and saying, "Look what I made!" is extremely hard and is objectively terrifying. Facing the public with the knowledge that the public won't always like us is a real and reasonable fear. That fear often locks us out of even starting the process and is what results in many authors whose writing is absolutely brilliant never seeing the success their art deserves.

Other than a few rare examples, I have not met a single author in all my years in the industry who doesn't feel that same way. We all experience the same discomfort, fear, and anxiety around being seen by the public. Our writing feels like parts of our souls laid bare, and being vulnerable in a world that is typically not at all gentle with such things is a very real difficulty. This includes bestselling authors at the top of the game, too. Yes, some people have massive egos, but as a general rule, we are all weird nerds in our PJ pants slamming away at the keys at all hours of the day.

I wanted to nod to this fear right at the outset of the marketing chapter because I know you're feeling it. I feel it, too. I've felt it every minute of my career. It's important to acknowledge and accept that we experience this. You aren't alone or uniquely bad or weak for feeling that way, either.

That said.

Marketing is not optional if you want to be successful. I have a dear friend of mine whose writing is absolutely stunning. Truly excellent. However, they cannot sell books for the life of them, so it doesn't seem to matter how many they have out, they aren't finding success as an author. That person just cannot seem to find their marketing legs, and it's been a source of constant frustration and misery.

I say this not to call that individual out, but because you are not alone in that experience if it's where you are. Just like feeling the fear of "I am being perceived!" is not something you are alone in. This stuff is *hard*, and there's no getting away from that. However, the only way out is through. If you want to be an author as a career, or even a profitable hobby, you are going to have to grab this bull by the horns and find your place.

When to Start Marketing

This is one of those questions that every author either asks or thinks they know the answer to when they start. Logic would suggest to most people that you start marketing when you have a book out because then you have something to sell, right?

Wrong.

You start marketing yourself the minute you decide you're going to do this seriously. Marketing isn't just advertising. You're looking to build brand awareness and get people to know you. To that end, marketing comes in three phases: pre-release, release, and post-release. If you don't have a book out yet, your pre-release will include different things than if you have books in print, but nonetheless, it'll be a similar principle.

Setting yourself up for success in the pre-release phase will support you through the others. However, if you already have a book out and are just reading this, recognize that books have a very, very long shelf life, so you aren't behind the curve if you already have a book out and are just now realizing you need to market it. The shelf life of a novel is like the half-life of that fruitcake Walmart sells around Christmas—which is to say, sometime between now and the heat death of the universe.

So what the heck do you do to market yourself if you don't have a product? A lot of the things in this chapter will still count. Setting up an author website, learning how to operate a mailing list, networking with authors and readers, getting your social media situation ironed out, and starting to talk about your project(s) is going to be your best bet. You might not have "fans" yet, but you can develop a pool of people who look forward to your book when it comes out, and you'll be creating a warm handoff.

Developing a presence on social media or other platforms will help you in the long run, and it's never too early to create one. Your posts don't need to be all sorts of magic, either. They can just be sharing bookish memes, your word count, and interacting with other writers in your community. Writers, after all, are almost inevitably readers, too, and we love supporting one another. I've purchased many books from authors I've become friends with.

In addition to that, once your book is heading toward publication (editing is done, and you're getting ready to upload, etc.), you'll want to really ramp up talking about your book and letting people know the next one is coming out. That energy and buzz will help you sell books during the release window and beyond.

Viewing Yourself as a Public Figure

Up until now, we've talked about business and thinking like a business person pretty extensively. Now we need to take the next step. While your books are absolutely a product you want to sell, the thing you are really trying to sell in all this is *yourself*. I don't mean in the OnlyFans way, though if you are doing OnlyFans, no shame to you. The thing is, your readers need to love your books, but with your books, they are going to associate these things with *you*.

This also means you are going to need to shift how you handle certain things. The minute you hit "publish," you become a public figure.

What this entails is considering how certain things might affect your image. This can include how you handle disputes on social media. I'm looking at a certain famous children's wizard school author who stuck her foot in it *hard* with the LGBTQIA+ community and has since become a villain in her own story. This also means considering your private social media space. When you become a public figure, you cannot assume the internet won't find out what you say on a private Facebook page.

You don't need to have everything in your life public. That's not at all what I'm suggesting here, so before you puff up like a scared cat, don't think your days of being able to eat Cheetos in your underpants while watching Netflix are over. Most of us won't be recognized in public or walk the red carpet.

However.

What you say online can come back to bite you. Hard. With that in mind, you need to think about and curate how personal you want to get on your Facebook feed, which you should be doing anyway, but still. You'll want to try and refrain from posting knee-jerk reactions to things online, getting into vicious flame wars, and being a jerk.

Yes, I know, you can be a jerk and still make money. There are plenty of rich jackasses out there who have followings I don't understand. But unless you aspire to be one of them, I recommend against being that kind of person.

I've also seen authors post long, whining, angry screeds about how their friends and family don't buy their books and how they're not real friends if they don't. Or people constantly bemoaning low sales (as in *constantly*). You can vent some of that in private with your friends and family, but I suggest strongly against doing it on your social media, even if you think your Facebook wall is private.

Moderating what you say and how you say it is an art form, and it takes time to figure that out for some folks. Transitioning from purely private social media use to handling being a public figure is not an easy adjustment, and a lot of folks stuff their feet in their mouths up to the kneecap or deeper.

You will make mistakes. I have made mistakes. When I do, I am honest, clear, and genuine in an apology. If I post something in error that is against who I am, then I am culpable for that. I also have changed as I've aged, so if someone dug back to a Facebook post from 2009 and saw that I said something at odds with who I am now, I'd shrug about it. Yes, I was a complete dingus when I was younger. Yes, I said some things I am not proud of now. No, I don't stand by them. It's okay to grow and change as a human. In fact, it's one of the best things about being human. I'm not who I was then, thankfully so.

Finally, please keep in mind that a pen name will not save you from this entirely. If you ever get big enough to make a serious impact, people will probably figure out who you are unless you put as much work into secrecy as Buckethead puts into his. At this point, that mystique is part of his brand.

In this day and age of reverse image searches, if you go to a public appearance or signing, someone can take your photo, put it into Google, and perform a search. If you've ever posted a photo online or had one posted of you, there's a good chance it'll pop up and recognize you. We live in that world. As authors, we need to do public events at times. So unless you want to go the Buckethead route, or Banksy, you need to make peace with that.

Creating Your Author Brand

The first thing that usually happens when I tell people they need to consider their branding is their eyes glaze over. Either that, or they freeze like a rabbit under a hawk's stare. If that's how you're feeling when reading that heading, it's okay. There's no huge secret to it, and you don't need to be afraid of this process.

Your author brand is nothing more or less than the parts of yourself that you want to share with the world. That's it. That's the whole thing. You can curate what you want to share and how much.

The second thing that happens is people immediately jump to, "I don't have anything to say that anyone would care about."

This is also wrong. You have plenty of things to say! You're an author, aren't you? Saying things is kind of our job.

In order to help you identify your brand, the first step is to take stock of interests you have that might relate to your book. For example, since I write urban fantasy, I definitely have an interest in *D&D* and other tabletop role-playing games (TTRPGs). So that's an easy one. I can talk about my TTRPGs and characters with no trouble at all. It's not deeply personal and is something people who read my books will probably like. Also, I play video games, particularly RPGs. Are we sensing a theme? So that's another thing I can discuss with readers.

You can continue this process on and on until you have a list of five or ten topics you think you might want to talk about to other people. Your brand can include as much or as little of your personal life as you want to share.

My brand includes disability, neurodivergence, TTRPGs, gaming, sword fighting, writing advice, humor, and crafting. I talk about those things on my social media pretty frequently both public-facing *and* private.

In that list, I can break it down further to individual topics I want to address, like the OGL disaster in the *D&D* community (if you know, you know). You can also use this to help you come up with blog posts, social media posts, short form video content... the possibilities are endless.

These branding elements should be things that connect to your target market (more on that later, don't panic yet), but if they're parts of you that you want to share, it'll connect with your audience. The thing is, though, you need to make sure they're *authentic*. These have to be things you genuinely get excited about or have feelings on. You shouldn't choose something you have no connection to because people will pick up pretty quickly on that and be turned off.

I know the "be yourself" advice is unhelpful, but in this way, it's true. Whatever your brand is, make sure you're honest about it. Be who you are, not who you think you should be. You don't need to be perfect, conventionally attractive, or any other specific thing in order to be successful. Most of us authors are strange little gremlin creatures subsisting on caffeine, chocolate, and quite probably cheese.

Don't deny it. You're among friends. We know.

Being your delightful, nerdy self is what the world needs, and it's what will come through in your writing. Being that person is a good and wonderful thing.

Why You Need a Website

Author websites are often one of the things people neglect the most. They think having social media profiles is sufficient, and I'm here to tell you it isn't. Your author website is going to be the hub of your wheel, and it's vital to have such a thing. If cost is a factor, you can substitute your own website with a free Wordpress.com account or something on Carrd or even a Substack until you can afford to have your own little corner of the internet. However, having your own website is one of the things you should pursue very early in your career.

The reasoning for this is that you own that patch of digital real estate, and no matter what happens, short of the internet going belly-up as a whole, you have that space. If social media all imploded tomorrow, you'd still have your website. It would be a way for readers to find and connect with you, much the same as your mailing list.

Your website doesn't need to be extremely complex. It can be as simple as you like but should contain a few key pieces:

- Your author name
- A small profile or bio about you

- Your books and where to buy them
- Your email
- Links to your social media

Those are the essentials. Your site might have other elements you want to include (mine shows off my fantasy mapmaking, for example), but you need to at least provide a space for fans and media folk to find you in order to connect with you.

It doesn't need to be updated constantly, either. It's essentially like your business card. Updating it by means of a blog or something can be a useful thing, though I prefer to blog on Substack, but it's not a requirement. Its function is just to create a place where folks can find you.

The Role of Social Media

If you hate social media, I'm not here to rub your nose in it. However, I do want to talk about social media and being an author because, like it or not, it can be a huge part of your author platform and gaining traction. It's not absolutely necessary, but in order to avoid it, you have to be willing to do all your marketing face to face. If the idea of talking to people about your book, attending local book events, and driving around to local bookstores to strike deals and do signings makes you break out in hives, social media may be a necessary evil.

The thing is that it's not the specifics of how you do it, but the reality that networking is going to be extremely important for your future sales. Whether you network online or in person is up to you, but you're still going to have to do it one way or another. Social media is just the easiest way to cast the widest net without spending money on it.

Back to focusing on social media. There are a few things you should really do when you first decide to publish. The first thing is to claim your author account name on all social media networks you can easily access. You don't need to *use* all these networks. The reason I say this is to prevent imposters as well as allow you the security to know your name is yours everywhere. Even if you're just digitally squatting on the real estate so nobody else can have it, it's an important thing to claim as a sort of insurance policy.

Once you've claimed your name everywhere, you should give some thought to which ones you actually want to use and how you want to use them. Not every author needs to be active on every social media network, and not every social media website will be where your target audience hangs out. Certain demographics use different platforms.

There's also the fact that you as a human being will not like or enjoy all social platforms. I, for example, *hate* X (Twitter). I find it constraining, stifling, and overwhelming—not to mention the moral issues with the platform these days. I am most comfortable on TikTok and Facebook. I also grudgingly use Instagram and LinkedIn and am on Discord far too frequently for my own good. I also have Threads and YouTube locked down, even if I'm not on them, as well as Tumblr. While I *do* have a Reddit account, I don't have one as an author at this point.

You can find whichever platforms you like best and dabble there. You aren't obligated to maintain an active presence on all of them. Play around a little and find the places you enjoy and are able to keep up with. If you hate and cannot keep up with the platform, you won't use it, and marketing will feel like death every time you have to do it.

On social media, your job is to connect with your audience while sticking with your brand. I post videos about writing advice on TikTok, share photos of my cats on Instagram, and talk about *D&D* on Facebook. I use them for different things and am gearing my content slightly differently on each platform. I didn't entirely do it on purpose, but that's how it came out in the wash.

The other thing is that you need to be active. That doesn't mean posting a hundred times a day. It just means popping in a few times a week or even once a day to check messages, post something, interact with people, and then off to do other things. I try to reply to every comment I receive unless it's something cruel or unhelpful.

I also go out of my way to engage on other people's pages. I find creators to comment on and tend to stick to encouragement rather than getting into the drama. All these paths are fair and doable. You just have to figure out which one is for you.

As I said at the start, social media doesn't need to be your marketing strategy if you'd rather be the kind of person who does things in person, but you do need to network one way or another.

Content Creation and Planning

If we are going to have social media outlets and other locations like a newsletter that we share regularly and engage with, we need to consider our content. This can be things like short-form videos, short-form writing (like Twitter), images, long-form writing (like blog posts or articles), excerpts from works you have in progress... anything, really, depending on your platforms. You are not locked into a specific kind of content creation to the exclusion of all others.

One of the nice things about content like this is we can plan it in advance. I have my blogs planned out several months in advance. My newsletter content, too. I keep all that in Plottr, my plotting program, and refer to it often. You can do the same with certain kinds of social media posts, like promotional content. Many platforms will allow you to schedule posts in advance, too. Or you could pay for a service like Hootsuite to do it for you.

This planning can be done once a week or once a month or even once every few months if you want to make a marathon of it. Then, once you have a plan, you can get to creating.

My usual method is to plan my posts out several months in advance and then choose one day a week to get all my content creation finished for things I have scheduled. That means the rest of the time, I can focus on other pursuits, like writing. If you get into the flow, it might only take you a couple hours, depending on how many pieces you need to plan and how long they are.

Planning and scheduling out your content in advance also takes some of the immediacy and anxiety out of the process. I can write my Substack articles for the month early on, schedule them, and then let them automatically go live. I do the same thing with my newsletter, which goes out twice a month. I also can batch create some visuals for my social media accounts for promotional purposes.

All these things are scheduled, planned, and known about in advance. They even go up and do their thing when I'm on vacation or not at my desk, so it's not obvious that I'm missing in action unless I tell people I'm going dark for a while.

If you have no idea what you'd ever say, I refer you back to our conversation about branding. Grab some of the topics that you said fit your brand and start there. You can also look to what holidays or observances are happening that month for ideas for timely content. Regardless of what format your content takes, you can develop it based on those ideas and set it up to share in advance. Then spend the rest of your time writing.

On occasion, you'll think of something you want to share or talk about in between, and that's a good moment to give people a little something extra.

As a final note regarding content, you need to make sure it's not exclusively sales-related. If your author social accounts read as one big advertisement for your book and reveal nothing about you, they won't connect with your readers as effectively. As a general rule, I shoot for 80% of my content to be something my audience connects with, finds funny, finds interesting, or somehow contributes to their day. 20% of my content is about sales. Now, you can certainly have it be that 80% of any individual post is about the topic and 20% of that post is sales. An example of this is me sharing a link to my books at the bottom of every newsletter but keeping the vast majority of the content to things that people will find interesting and enjoy.

This holds true for things like YouTube videos, too. You can have a fifteen-minute video that's got a two-minute plug for your books at the end, or one minute. Either way, you can add a short promotion to many types of media without being obnoxious about it. The key is to remember that marketing is about *connection*. Advertising is part of marketing, but not all marketing is advertising. Building a community and developing relationships is a large part of marketing, and if all you do is ask them to do things for you when you aren't doing anything for them, it's not a two-way street.

The Value of Newsletters

There are people in the world who will tell you email marketing is obsolete and worthless. They will try and convince you that only social media marketing matters, and things like owning your mailing list aren't important.

Those people are wrong.

Newsletters are like author websites: They're something you *own*. While you might not own the platform you use (I use MailerLite), the list of emails of people you email to is yours forever unless someone unsubscribes from your newsletter. That's important in an age where social media platforms can be unstable (X/Twitter) or the fate of them can be uncertain (TikTok). Social pages can also be hacked and stolen. I've heard of authors who were locked out of their Facebook pages and groups by people they were working with, and then lost *everything*.

If that sends a cold shiver down your spine, it should. It's terrifying.

Newsletters are a way you can connect with your readers that you have complete control over. Their value is in that it's your space, uncluttered with advertisements and information trying to drag the reader's attention elsewhere. It's a little space that's just you and them.

You can also set it up to go out as frequently or infrequently as you like. I have mine go out twice a month at the moment, but if I wanted to drop it to monthly, I could do that. I went with twice a month because it felt good to me. Some people who have more coming out or are doing non-fiction have their newsletter come out weekly. The only wrong answer here is to exclusively send out emails on release days for both technical reasons (you might well get flagged as spam) and because readers will forget who you are, why they signed up, and will likely either mark you as spam or delete the email unread.

My friend, Tammi Lebrecque, wrote an excellent pair of books on newsletters that I highly suggest you read. The series is called *Newsletter Ninja*, and she has both brass tacks help in what to do with your newsletter and broader scope elements that will give you information on things like how to write and design a reader cookie and what that is. I'm not going to attempt to duplicate Tammi's work here and instead will encourage you to read more in-depth on the subject in her books.

The Introversion Crisis

As I said at the start of the chapter, authors tend to be introverts. That's just it. We typically want to be left to our own devices or daydream rather than interact with other humans. Often, we do so grudgingly and try to limit it as much as possible. This is one of the few near-universal truths of being an author.

Unfortunately for us, making money at our chosen vocation requires us to interact with *people*. And it requires it quite a lot. I frequently hear authors talk about how they're too introverted to market or talk about their books, too introverted to participate in writing groups, and too introverted to attend author events.

Look, as an introverted autistic person, I get it. Down in my bones, I get it. My natural habitat is in my fuzzy, teal bathrobe burritoed in as many fluffy things as I can magpie from around the house, doing my own thing in my corner of the room while my husband does his thing in his corner of the room. My ideal life involves very limited socializing with a very small number of people.

However, reality doesn't much care what my ideal life would be, and I also know that if nobody knows I've written a book, I'll never be able to sell the fool thing. Whether you go traditional or self-publishing, all roads lead to marketing, and you can't be successful if you aren't willing to push outside the bubble on a semi-regular basis in certain ways.

Nobody expects us to be extroverts. If they do, they have never met an author in real life and have some dire misconceptions about what we do and who we are. We do, however, need to maintain a presence somehow.

For me, my most comfortable spaces are online. I get to interact but also put my phone down or turn off my computer and walk away. I attend virtual seminars and networking events, I attend virtual conferences and in-person ones when I can, and talk to other authors.

It gets easier with time. I would advise starting with small things outside your comfort zone. Join and regularly interact with one writing group. Maybe attend one virtual seminar. Do things a piece at a time to build up your tolerance to do more. You might never be comfortable with all the pieces that come with being out in public, but you might be able to tolerate it for longer without coming apart.

Whatever your one thing is, start there and keep at it. Then add a second. Before you know it, you'll be able to do more than you expected. And since you're not on anybody's timeline but your own, you can take as much time as you need to at each stage as long as you're still working and not growing complacent. After all, you can't go to the gym once and expect immediate transformation. It takes time and work, and as the work grows easier, you add more weight.

Interacting with Fans

This is one of the areas I see authors stumble in frequently. Some authors treat fans like ATMs and tend to get haughty or self-important about the whole writing deal. That's not how I would like to be treated as a person, so it's certainly not how I'd treat fans. On the other hand, some folks treat fans as terrifying apparitions worthy of *A Christmas Carol*. I understand that since the idea of someone being a fan of mine is a little terrifying. I live in my own head and struggle with the idea of people getting excited to meet or talk to me. However, I can't really let my fans know that because projecting confidence is one of the things that matters.

So how do we do it?

Well, if someone approaches us to talk, the first thing you'll want to do is thank them. Thank them for reading, thank them for enjoying your story, or whatever it is. Appreciate them in return. Then listen to them and let them talk a little. If they ask questions about your books, answer them! If you stick your foot in your mouth, apologize.

That's one of the big things, too. If you screw up—and you will, we are all humans—the thing is to apologize. Certain authors—like the Author Who Shall Not Be Named who wrote a series of books about a boy wizard—seem allergic to the idea of apologies. When you make a mistake, rather than getting your hackles up, be honest and apologize. It's okay to make mistakes. We all do it. If someone walked up to me and told me I'd written something that harmed them, my immediate reply would be to apologize.

Unless, of course, they're a bigot upset with me writing about LGBTQIA+ people or something. In which case they can find a pier and launch themselves off it, please and thank you.

I interact with people who I have met because they are fans of my work on a semi-regular basis. In fact, some of them have become good friends and become beta readers or ARC reviewers for me in time. I've had folks reach out and tell me they loved my characters, and I've been thrilled to hear it. When people respond to my email newsletter, I do my best to take time and reply. The same with social media.

If someone is taking the time to comment on your post, reply to your email, or otherwise send you a message letting you know they appreciate you? That's gold right there. Be gracious, be thankful, and be genuine. I've had people send me fan art of my characters, even, and my heart always does an excited little back flip in my chest. When people I know want me to sign their copy of my book, I do a little wiggle. It's magic.

Never forget that magic. Never let it become humdrum. Enjoy their gratitude and appreciate their time and attention because without it, we are just people staring at a screen and hallucinating for hours. I don't mean to insult people who write for personal pleasure; creating art for art's sake does have value. But for those of us who are looking to publish our books and earn a living from that venture, the people who read our works are really the folks we need to thank for having that opportunity.

Summary

Marketing is the single most dreaded element of being an author whenever I speak with authors. It's a large subject and the one that feels the least like it fits with our typically introverted selves. There are a lot of moving parts and a lot of things you can try and play with to develop your personal marketing strategy. That strategy will have a direct effect on your book sales, but the good news you can change it at any time and see what works and what doesn't without ruining your career.

While you cannot avoid marketing wholesale, you can definitely decide what makes the most sense for you, your book, and your personality. The only wrong way to market will be the way that doesn't work—much like the other advice in this book.

Key Takeaways

- Marketing is a constant element of our lives as authors. We need to be consistently letting folks know we and our books exist. This process can start before you have a single book in print, too!

- Being a public figure can feel daunting for people whose work has them spending many hours in isolation staring at a screen. However, it is a skill you can learn and a mindset you can achieve if you work at it.

- Ensuring you have a website and social media profiles set up for yourself as your public face is an important part of marketing your books. While you can choose which outlets to pursue, you will need to create at least some kind of presence online, and at the very least you must have an author website.

- Developing content for your website or social media profiles is a never-ending thing but doesn't have to be excessively onerous. Spending a day a week planning your posts and strategy can be enough for many people. You don't need to post every minute of every day.

- Newsletters are still valuable, still important, and still sell books even in today's age where they often feel like a dinosaur. They're a more personal way for readers to connect with you and are a powerful tool in your sales toolbox.

- Interacting with your fans is hard and can be intimidating. Knowing how to keep your private self private while sharing some parts of your life is a delicate dance. As is ensuring you aren't oversharing to strangers. Ultimately, remember that whatever you say to others as your author self is representing your brand, not just you.

- It is tempting to hide in a hole and not market because it's a frightening thing for many authors. Unfortunately, the path to success absolutely requires marketing, and that cannot be avoided. However you decide to market is fine, but it is an utter necessity.

Chapter Twelve

Finding Your Target Audience

Now that we've addressed some of the basics of marketing, let's dig deeper into it. This is something I've alluded to through this book, but we're going to get up to our eyeballs in this in a minute. However, the core of this chapter is based around one question: Who is going to read my book?

This question is often associated with fear because we find ourselves inadequate or frustrated since we haven't the faintest idea. Knowing who you are writing for and who is going to read your book is one of those things that can provoke the "how should I know; I'm not psychic!" response in us. While that is true to some extent, you don't need to be a mind reader to identify your target audience.

In this chapter, I'm going to give you some concrete suggestions on how you can find these people you want to work with and how to deliver things they are interested in. You may discover it's not as hard as you think.

Identifying Your Target Audience

This term is going to come up a lot through the course of this chapter, and it's important to explain it early on so you don't develop misconceptions about it or worry. Identifying your target market isn't extremely difficult and can honestly be a fun process.

In a nutshell, your target audience—also called your "target market"—is the people who will enjoy your book. Many people make the mistake of thinking "everyone" is their target market, so disabuse yourself of that notion right now. You can't market to "everyone" because it'll be the equivalent of yelling "buy my stuff" while you're in the pit at a Metallica concert. Nobody's going to hear you, and they're also not there for that. They're there to see Metallica.

If you're not sure who the heck this target audience is at all, start with a few key factors: age, genre, and gender. I know it seems very backwards to target gender, but some things appeal more strongly to one audience than another based on gender norms. The point here isn't to say nobody who isn't your target audience will enjoy your book, either. You're trying to get closest to identifying who *will* enjoy your book.

If the above questions don't seem to help, consider working backwards. Who do you think your book *won't* be for? Let's do some examples.

I'm going to be making some gender associations here based on the way things currently are. This is not saying they *should* be this way. I am non-binary and firmly believe that gender is a social construct and has very little meaning for me. That said, I am not going to ignore the fact that the social construct has impact in ways I need to account for.

These constructs can change, and they likely will. What was true about men and women even thirty years ago is changing, so make sure you look at how things are now rather than wishing they were different. Your target market means people who exist right now under the current social norms.

We're back to *Star Wars* again. It was only a matter of time.

If I had to think about the kinds of people who probably wouldn't be into *Star Wars: Episode IV*, I'd start by saying the movies are in English (not counting translations; we're pretending those haven't been done to simplify this). If someone cannot speak or understand English, then they probably won't want to watch *Star Wars* with me right now. That cuts out a huge percentage of people on the planet.

Next, people who really think fiction is a waste of time (and they exist) won't enjoy *Star Wars*. They'll think it's campy and not worth it. So that's another swath of the population gone. Then we have people who would think the idea of space wizards is an affront to their religious beliefs. That's a third group out. Then there are children who couldn't understand it or would find it frightening, so probably nobody under the age of eight or nine is really going to *get* it. I started watching it when I was around two, but you get my point.

You can see where this is going. You can remove large groups from your pool of your target market without much effort. As you do that, you begin to see more of who might enjoy your book.

For simplicity's sake, I am going to assume this movie was coming out *now* rather than nearly forty years ago (ouch, that hurt to write). I am also going to presume an English-only release on launch.

- Men between 8 and 20
- People who enjoy science fiction
- English speakers
- Western (geopolitical, not genre) audiences
- Nerds and geeks
- Fantasy lovers who are open to sci-fi

Leia doesn't become the feminist icon she is until later movies, so this movie as a stand-alone is a save-the-princess movie. The first trilogy of movies (*IV, V, VI*) are also very much written by and for the male gaze. Women/AFAB folks were *not* the target audience. I still love the movies. I have a deep and abiding love for *Star Wars*. No questions asked. However, I also have to acknowledge that I was not the target market for those movies.

Acknowledging these things doesn't mean you are omitting potential readers who will enjoy your book, either. My novels are written in a more "masculine" manner than a "feminine" manner, which means they'll draw more masculine folks. However, I have a large number of female readers who adore them.

What you're doing with this process is not just cutting out people who wouldn't enjoy it, but targeting markets who will. When you target that market, you will catch places it overlaps. Back to *Star Wars*. I'm not male, between the ages of 8 and 20, or a dedicated science fiction fan. I am, however, a Western English speaker, a nerd, and a fantasy lover who is open to science fiction (Anne McCaffrey gets me). As such, I am a Venn Diagram with a number of these key points. Or, as a dear friend of mine would call it, "a messy stack of pancakes."

Keep in mind, too, that your target market might change depending on the book, the series, or the times. People who were really into one thing at one time might shift into another demographic, just like how pink was a masculine color, then a hyper-feminine color, and now it's returning to neutral. That's okay. Marketing is not a zero-sum game, and you can change things up whenever you need to.

Creating Your Reader Avatar

A "reader avatar" is essentially the personification of your target market. I'll explain this in more detail as we go, but think of this person as the exact individual you know needs or will love your book. The reason we get so specific about this is that, when you market to a very specific person—or a group of traits if you don't want to anthropomorphize them—it's throwing a boulder into a puddle versus throwing a grain of sand into the ocean.

I know as writers, we like to think that our books are for "everyone." We hope everybody will love our content, and we rightfully are optimistic about that! However, we need to be real. No matter what genre and subject matter you're writing about, there are people who just plain would not read and enjoy your book.

For writers who have no idea who your book is *for*, the start of the process can be identifying who the book absolutely isn't for. I'm going to give you the breakdown I used of this very book series and share the process with you so you can execute it for your own books. I am also going to include it for my urban fantasy series, *Boston Blight*. Non-fiction is a little easier to do this for than fiction, but the process is the same overall.

Rather than wandering about in the desert, I think it'll make the most sense to just get straight to it and show you how this works rather than explain it first.

Non-Fiction

For this book series, *Finish the Damn Book*, I'm going to break down who this book isn't for first. It removes broad swaths of the population in quick strokes, too.

This book series isn't for: people who aren't interested in writing and publishing books; people looking for deep advice on specific craft points; experienced authors who don't need this kind of guidance; people who don't like my sense of humor; individuals looking to make a "quick buck" on writing.

As you can see, that cut out a huge number of people very quickly. If someone doesn't care about writing and publishing books, they're never going to want to read these books. It's not going to be an area of interest whatsoever to them. I'm not going to try and attract people who aren't looking for what I'm selling. So, with who this *isn't* for out of the way, let's start tackling who it *is* for.

This book series is for: new and emerging authors who want to finish a book and don't know how to go about publishing; people who like that information to come with snarky humor and bad jokes; people who are serious about putting the work in on the business of their books and publishing career; individuals who might want to work with me as an editor (yes, I take clients to help with all this stuff!); people who find the idea of publishing overwhelming and need help and prefer straightforward, no-nonsense advice.

Now, you can absolutely stop there, but I like to go a step further and create a whole human being to market to. That is partially because I really enjoy character design, but it's *also* an exercise in being less intimidated by marketing.

I'm not speaking to just a faceless collection of abstracts. I'm speaking to a human. Just one human, too.

So, using the above information, let's create our ideal author avatar for the non-fiction book series you're reading right now! I'm going to name them Morgan because this book series is not specifically for a gender, and Morgan's a lovely, gender-neutral name. (Rowan is another favorite of mine. And Charlie.)

Morgan has been writing all their life and really loves it. They want to pursue a career as an author but aren't sure how to go about it. They've just graduated with a degree in creative writing, but their teachers didn't really give them the details on how to move forward. They know the craft end of writing pretty well, or at least have a good grasp of it, but they have no idea what to do with a manuscript when it's finished. Heck, Morgan's barely written a full book. In fact, all they have is a collection of short stories from their last year in school. They're great stories, but they don't have a novel, and that's what they want to write. Morgan has two cats, works as a barista at a local coffee shop, and spends way too much time there after work writing because it's the place where words flow best for them.

Now that we've created Morgan, my marketing content can be focused to them. Morgan has cats and enjoys animal companions (many writers have pets, so this is taking from actual data). That means sharing animal photos or stories of my pets is going to be a hit with them. I regularly include pet content in my newsletter. Also, Morgan's probably a coffee addict (again, a lot of writers are). I am not a coffee addict—I prefer tea—but I can relate to enjoying a warm drink. And I can share coffee memes that I know will hit home with this audience.

I'm not going to regale you with every element of my personal marketing plan for this book here, but you can see how the reader avatar works and what its function is. I'm not making content for "everyone." I'm making content for Morgan.

Fiction

It's a little different with fiction, but not much. For this segment, I'm going to pivot to talking about my urban fantasy thriller book series, *Boston Blight*. By the end of this exercise, if you're one of the people who enjoys this kind of book, I'll have done my job right.

Boston Blight is NOT for: people offended by LGBTQIA+ characters; people who want a lot of steamy content in their books; people looking for a romantic read; people who are offended by frank discussions of religion (the good, the bad, and the ugly); people who don't like angels and demons as characters; people who don't enjoy fantasy; people who don't like thrillers; people who don't like modern settings; people who don't want to see a non-binary lead character; people who don't like first person POV.

I'm sure I could keep going for the next five hundred years, but you get the picture. And by the list of who it's *not* for, you can see it's starting to shape who the books *are* for. But, just to continue and finish this off...

Boston Blight is for: people who liked *Lucifer*, *Supernatural*, *Good Omens*, and *Sandman*; people who enjoy LGBTQIA+ representation; Christians engaging in deconstruction; people who aren't religious but can enjoy stories that contain it; readers who enjoyed *The Dresden Files* and *The Iron Druid Chronicles*; readers of thrillers; people who don't require romance be the primary story; people looking for a book series and don't mind waiting for it to finish.

Okay, we have our data points. But who is our avatar? I'm going to go with a male name since my target audience isn't female, though there are plenty of women who will absolutely enjoy these books—more on that later. I think I'm going to go with Alexander. I love that name.

Alexander is twenty-eight years old, has a cat, and is bisexual. He really loved Lucifer *and enjoyed most of the seasons of* Supernatural. *He doesn't have a huge amount of time, so doesn't want to read massive epics, but he does enjoy reading. He thinks he might be neurodivergent but isn't necessarily sure. He relates to a lot of the content he sees on TikTok. Alexander is also a tabletop gaming nerd who spends a lot of time daydreaming about his characters and their stories. He's a bit of a history nerd and has a sword he wants to put up on the wall, but it currently lives in his closet.*

Okay, Alex sounds like a sweetheart, and I kind of want to give him a hug! If I'm making content that's targeting him, which my content absolutely would, that means it'll gather people like him.

Finally, let's get into the last piece of the reader avatar. A lot of folks balk at the idea of being so specific because they think it will exclude people who aren't Morgan or Alex specifically. That couldn't be further from the truth. Content that Morgan and Alex relate to will also strike chords with folks who are into the same things they are. If my book reaches a forty-something who has always wanted to write but never had the chance, they'll probably find my content helpful and useful, just like Morgan. If my fiction runs across the TikTok feed of someone who is a gamer and enjoys diverse casts of characters, then they'll definitely enjoy my series.

Creating a very specific avatar and a very specific vision of who your work is *for* means it'll catch everyone who is near it. That also means you won't have to waste time, money, and effort trying to market to people who will never in a million years want the product you're selling.

It's like Facebook ads trying to sell me makeup. Look, I might be AFAB ("assigned female at birth," if you don't recognize the term), but I loathe it. And no amount of them spending money to try and sell me makeup is going to work. However, it *has* figured out that Kickstarter tabletop games will get me to click every time. We aren't going to talk about my game room and my game book addiction. *Shh.*

If you create a very specific idea of who your work is for and market to that effectively and well, you will naturally draw in everyone adjacent to that. And of course, people who aren't in your immediate target market will eventually find your book—that goes without question. However, marketing often involves money, and I don't want to pay my hard-earned coin to put my advertising in front of people who will soak up the advertising budget but never, ever buy.

Connecting with your target audience

Once you've identified with your target audience, who might look an awful lot like you in some ways, then you need to think about how to connect with them. Marketing is about *connection*. Hands down, every time I talk about marketing, I will talk about connection. The thing is, too, that connection is a genuine thing. It's not random or faked or forced. It's about forging honest relationships—even if they're shallow ones—between your brand, you as an author, and your readers.

Reading is an intimate experience between author and reader. You are seeing pieces of someone else's soul and heart, and the longer you spend reading a particular author, the more of a connection you likely feel to that person. I grew up thinking of Anne McCaffrey as almost an aunt who gave amazing advice and told beautiful stories. I lived in the *Pern* books as a kid. When we're talking marketing, we're talking about that kind of connection. Even if you don't personally know all your fans—and I hope you have enough of them that you can't know them all personally!—they will want to know you and feel connected to you.

If that sounds terrifying, don't worry. Take a deep breath. You don't need to share your darkest secrets or give details about every part of your life to your fans. You are allowed to have privacy and things you don't share. Remember what I said in the Marketing Principles chapter about branding: It's what parts of yourself you *choose* to share with the world.

If, like me, you're a dedicated introvert who was the odd man out in school forever (being neurodivergent will do that), connection is stressful, and we often have no idea how to go about doing it. Fortunately, in marketing, it's not hard. One of the first things you want to think about is what emotions you want people to feel when interacting with your content.

When I'm producing marketing content for my various outlets about my editing and publishing work, the emotions I'm trying to elicit are trust, curiosity, inspiration, and a feeling of self-empowerment. I want the people who see my videos, read my newsletter, and read my books to trust me. In order for you to apply the principles I lay out, you need to have faith in the fact that I know what I'm doing and have any reason to be giving you this advice. Also that I'm not trying to just steal your money and promise you things I can't deliver.

So how do I go about inspiring those feelings?

I can only speak for myself, but the way I approach it is by being transparent, honest, direct, clear, and warm. Or at least, I try to be. I don't pull punches about things that don't work and have sharp criticism for a lot of practices that I view as harmful or damaging to an author's career. (There's a lot of *truly* atrocious advice out there.) However, I also try and give people the data to back it up. I've been in the publishing industry for sixteen years as I write this, which is no small amount of time, and the information I have has been corroborated repeatedly by folks with way more experience than I have. So I am acting in good faith when I share it.

I also don't hide who I am. I am a neurodivergent, queer, non-binary, disabled person. That is all over my social media and content. I'm not saying you are required to out yourself as anything that isn't safe for you. You very much are not. I want you to stay safe and taken care of no matter what stage of life you are in and whoever you are. But for me? I am out and I am loud about it to ensure people feel safe with me. Or, at least the people I *want* to feel safe with me.

These things are choices.

Connecting with your audience is about being authentic to yourself. If you really love model trains? Tell people you really love model trains. Find your people and share with them. Are you a hiker? A knitter? A *huge* fan of that one show? Share some of these things with the people you're reaching out to. Let them feel that connection to you as a human being.

The other thing that really makes a difference with feeling connected to people is engaging with them. I reply to as many comments on my social media as I can. I respond to emails and DMs. I am grateful when people take time to talk to me, and I do my best to reciprocate. There are times when it's not possible to give a personal response to everyone. I had a video go viral a little while back. As I write this, it's at over a million views and thousands of comments. I couldn't give a personal reply to every single comment. I would be both overwhelmed and probably want to delete the social media app altogether. Instead, I "liked" everyone's comments that I saw that weren't unkind and responded to people who asked questions or said something deeply heartfelt or personal. I tried to show people I care.

Regardless of the forum, if someone reaches back to you, engage with them. I've made some wonderful friends that way and fostered strong relationships with people I never would have met otherwise. I have also made some superfans' day, week, and month by talking to them and sending them photos of my cats.

Finally, you need to also engage with other people. Whether you're doing social media, Substack, a newsletter... Find your people and engage with them. Talk to other authors, talk to other fans of the media you love, and participate in communities. This is not, of course, to the exclusion of your writing time, but it is absolutely a part of your marketing time. Jim Butcher, author of the *Dresden Files*, is a member of the same reenactment group I'm in. If I ever met him at an event, I would love to cross swords with him. He's a fencer, I believe.

Also, I want to send his son a message and my book and tell him we need to duel on Boston Common for the right to write in Boston. We're both using that setting for urban fantasy books, and I feel like a duel is the only way to settle it properly. By duel, I mean... we wear safety gear, abide by rules, and poke each other for giggles, then write our series anyway, of course.

It might feel terrifying or undesirable at first. However, if we want to sell books, we need to find ways to step outside of that and make genuine connections with others, even if you do so on your terms and in your ways. You don't need to force yourself to do specific things that are terrible for you. However, you *do* need to find ways to connect with people in whatever form that takes.

To Niche Down or Not

Before we get into the meat of this, I want to explain what I mean because overexplaining is my thing. Yay, autism.

In this context, I'm specifically talking about your marketing niche, not your writing niche. I cover the writing one in the first book in this set, so if you'd like to know more about *that*, I encourage you to pick that one up. When it comes to marketing, there are a couple mindsets. Both of them have borne fruit for authors of various types, so I'm not here to tell you to ascribe to a specific one. Instead, I want to lay both of the options out to you so you can consider what the best path is for you.

The first school of thought is that your marketing should be laser-focused on *only* your books and content that supports them. This is visible in a lot of spheres, but I'm going to point toward TikTok a little, particularly romance authors. No, I am not picking on romance authors in general; y'all just do this specific thing really well on TikTok, so I'm calling it out. What these authors do is create short videos with strong hooks that get people to have an emotional response that draws them into buying the book. Other genres do this, too, but romance and erotica are, by a *dramatic* margin, the ones that make this technique work for them. I haven't seen much traction from other genres using this technique on TikTok, but I've seen it in action on many non-fiction author pages and communities. I know it's not *just* romance or *just* TikTok.

This method of marketing requires you to have a strong and one-track focus on just your books and what they do well. When doing that, you talk about literally nothing but your book or things adjacent to it. This can also look like romance authors who make those marketing videos but also only do content specifically about their books and don't address much of anything else.

The *other* school of thought is the one I use because the first method just does not work for me as a person. I don't think that way, run out of content in about five seconds, and then have a meltdown. In the other school of thought, you can make content about a constellation of specific things. For me, it's neurodivergence, TTRPG stuff, history, disability, LGBTQIA+, and writing/editing.

With the second school of thought, you cast a broader net and have more things to discuss, but it does require more work in the sense that you can't just recycle hooks or videos as well and need to put more thought into the content more consistently.

In essence, to be honest, one is really focused on marketing a product, and the other is more focused on marketing a person. Both are effective, and both can be excellent for different minds. You can also use one type of marketing in one place and do another on another platform. It's all about figuring out what is going to work best for your books, you as an author, and for the platform(s) you prefer. What works on one doesn't necessarily work on another.

Also, different genres have different levels of success with these two methods. My only specific knowledge of that is anecdotal, however, so I am not going to do more than say that you should see what successful authors in your genre are doing and pull out of those techniques the things that work for you as an individual human.

Why You Can't Please Everyone

This is a reality for us as authors and for humans at large. We cannot please everyone who will read our books. It's pointing back to that target audience situation but also acknowledging that even then, there will be people in our target audience we cannot make fully happy with everything. Speaking from a diversity, equity, and inclusion angle (DEI), there's also the reality that no group is a monolith, so even different subgroups will feel differently about various pieces.

I am going to discuss something not immediately and directly writing-related, but it ties in, I promise. You also don't need to have a horse in the race I'm going to bring up as an example, so please understand that this is a situation to illustrate that not everyone can be pleased. It's not commentary about this specific situation. Well, not entirely.

As a disabled, autistic person, I am very aware that there are several schools of thought regarding how we refer to ourselves or how others refer to us. There is one school of thought who voraciously advocates for "person-first language." That is to say, they believe strongly that I am a "person who is autistic" or a "person who is disabled." The thought process behind this is to emphasize my personhood over anything else. This school of thought has also headed into other realms, such as a "person of color" versus "non-white person."

The other school of thought is "identity-first language," which puts the identity at the head of the sentence. You might have gleaned above which one I fall into by context, but the "identity-first language" model would label me as a disabled person or an autistic person. To some, this de-emphasizes my personhood and gives weight to the "label." Personally, I am of the belief that, if I have to remind you I am a *person* before anything else, then we have a whole host of problems that rephrasing a sentence isn't going to solve.

There are also other linguistic nuances like the fact that identity-first language is fine unless it's something that's "bad." You say someone's an "artist" not a "person who creates art."

Now, I mention this because the disabled community is not a monolith. There are people in good faith on both sides of the discussion who have *very* strong feelings about it. Even if I am representing disabled characters in a positive and non-ableist light to the best of my ability, I cannot please everyone. If I call them disabled people, the person-first language people might grimace. If I do it the other way around, the identity-first language folks will sigh and roll their eyes.

This is, however, a far lesser issue than whether or not I'm representing disabled people in a positive light in my series, which I am. But no matter what I do or how I bend myself into a pretzel, I will never please *both* groups of people fully.

I am at peace with that.

You will need to make similar decisions about your works, too. You will not be able to make everyone happy, even if it's people who are on the same side of an issue or part of the same community. It's not your job as a writer to make *everybody* happy. It's your job to act in good faith, do your best to do right, and tell good stories.

How this ties into marketing, and why it's in this chapter, is because you will encounter comments like this on social media and in reviews. There are people who will give you lower reviews because of something that is purely personal preference that has no impact on how you write your series. There are people who will leave grouchy or downright mean comments on social media posts they disagree with. This is inevitable. Even Fred Rogers (Mister Rogers) had detractors who didn't like him.

I'm not advocating that you give everyone the middle finger and say, "I don't care what you think, I'm doing my thing." That's an attitude a lot of people take in the face of this reality, and it's not a healthy one. You should *care* about these decisions, particularly when they're important ones dealing with marginalized individuals or other such sensitive subjects. However, if you study and think and remain teachable and make decisions in good faith, you will have a far stronger case.

There's also the fact that, when we do stick our foot in something and do something that harms people by mistake or ignorance, we must remain teachable. Be honest. If you screw up, own it. I point you toward the musician, Lizzo, who used the word "spaz" in her song lyrics, entirely unaware that it was a pejorative term to folks with neurological disorders. When it was called to her attention, she apologized wholeheartedly and corrected the song lyrics.

Now, not all of us will be able to rewrite our books if we accidentally say or do something like that. We might have a stickier situation than just changing one word in a song or doing a find-and-replace for a word that upset folks. How we choose to handle it at that point is a matter of what we are feasibly able to do in good faith. Can we fix the problem without destroying a long-running series? Can we add a blog post or disclaimer somewhere saying we are aware of the situation, but we cannot go back and rewrite things to fix it? Are we able to fix it moving forward?

Those are all solid questions to ask ourselves about what we're going to do in a situation like that. We also need to evaluate the situation itself. Are we actually in the wrong, or is this a situation like the person-first and identity-first language above, where communities are not monoliths? Have we thought the thing through and made an informed decision in good faith?

We cannot please everyone. That is actual hard fact. However, we can do our best to be thoughtful, considerate, and teachable without sacrificing our artistic integrity.

Summary

As authors, our target audiences are often people very much like us. After all, we write books we enjoy reading! Locating and connecting with your target audience can feel like some mammoth, complicated, terrifying thing, but really it's just about finding people with similar hobbies and interests to yourself. It's also about connecting with people who are passionate about the subjects of your book.

Key Takeaways

- Figuring out who your target audience is will allow you to market your book to those people who already want a book just like yours. You won't be screaming into a void trying to out-compete others. You will be telling people who want what you have that your work exists.

- Building a reader avatar for a book is a very helpful exercise that can give you a clearer image of your target audience and take away some of the anxiety. You don't need to market to some massive, faceless crowd; you can market to a specific individual who represents the people you want to connect with.

- Connecting with your target audience means being honest, genuine, and real. You do not need to be fake and false in order to market your books. In fact, the more real and genuine you are, the better you will connect with the individuals you want reading your books.

- Choosing to niche down into a very targeted market can be a very good idea for certain books and certain authors. For others it will limit you in ways that may not be helpful. Making this decision with clarity of focus is important. Choosing your niche(s) is also an important part of this process.

- Understanding that being an author comes with rejection—as we went over before—is part of the whole process. You cannot and will not be able to please everyone. It's okay that your book isn't going to be beloved by literally everybody. That doesn't mean you're doing something wrong.

Chapter Thirteen

Social Media for Authors

Many of us, if not most of us, use social media these days. If you don't and have no desire to, then this may not be the chapter for you. However, I strongly advise that you give that thought deep consideration. Even if you don't use social media for any personal purposes whatsoever, having it for your author presence is worth considering. The benefits of it far outweigh the drawbacks for most people.

All that said, I don't want to encourage people to do something that will be damaging for their mental health, so if you really think being on social media will harm you, don't do it.

Finding Places to Be

Social media is, in a word, overwhelming. There are so many options from X (Twitter) to TikTok to Mastadon to Reddit and so on. It's easy to panic and shut down when faced with the massive range of possibilities when it comes to social media platforms you have use of as an author. The good news is, you don't need to *use* all of them, though I again strongly suggest claiming a username on each of them that, preferably, is the same username or one very close thereto.

Claiming your name on all the platforms is essentially digital squatting. It prevents people from creating an account and pretending to be you using a name you have branded. I don't advocate you trying to utilize all the platforms that exist out there if you ever want to write again, but owning an account on the major ones isn't a bad idea on principle.

From there, you need to consider three specific questions to help guide you toward which social media method you want to employ as your primary:

- Which social media platform are you the most comfortable using and enjoy the most, even if you don't necessarily enjoy it fully?

- Which social media platform does your target audience hang out on?

- What platform(s) do you think you could use most consistently and find the least disruptive to your daily life?

Social media is a reality for authors unless you want to go down the traditional route of going to in-person events, traveling, and hand-selling your book. That absolutely can be a route that works for people, but it also has its drawbacks: Booths at events aren't cheap, gas is expensive, and in-person events require a lot of time and energy. Social media is here to stay, much as we might long for the days before its existence or want MySpace back. Seriously. Tom, where are you?

If you get that joke, make sure you take some anti-inflammatories for your back and tell the kids to get off your lawn.

Choosing which platform(s) to haunt is a matter of knowing what you like most as well as where your identified market hangs out. The answer as to where your market hangs out is easily found. Do some internet searches for what social media company demographics are, and you'll find them. I'm not going to give you more specific data on which platform appeals to who because, by the time you read this, the demographics could be different. Your best bet is to look up what's current to you now. Also, there may be social media companies that aren't invented yet at the time I'm writing this guide.

Right now, my primary social media for my author work is TikTok. It's my biggest and most active platform, and it's the one I enjoy the most. I find X (Twitter) toxic and overwhelming, by and large. I use Facebook for networking, much like LinkedIn, but I don't do much actual marketing on there. I do some, but the majority of my target market isn't on Facebook, which suits me just fine. I find shouting into the void on my author Facebook page disheartening since organic traffic is so low on there that I almost forget the page exists a majority of the time.

Just as I have my preferences, so too will you develop your own. It's okay to dabble in various social media places to see what you like and what you don't, too. You don't need to pick one and stick with it forever. If a new one comes along, you can pop onto it and see what you think of it before deciding if it's going to be your thing.

Social Media Etiquette for Public Figures

This segment exists because I have seen a lot of people shoot themselves in the foot so many times, their leg was missing to the knee. While I rarely give hard and fast rules in anything I do, I have some serious warnings that I want to be crystal clear about when it comes to how you behave in public.

The first thing you need to know is that your public-facing social media profiles should *not* be treated like your personal ones. It requires an entirely different mindset because what you can do in private is different from how you should conduct yourself in public. However, you must also be aware that your private social media pages are not impervious, and if you have anything on them that is controversial, or you say things in public groups or threads that are, you are not immune to backlash. I mentioned this in an earlier segment, and it's worth saying again here. That's how strongly I feel about it.

Making sure you have that clear and bright line between personal profile and public profiles is of extreme importance. There are things you can get away with as a private individual that you should avoid like the plague as a public figure.

So, what are my rules for using social media as a public figure? Let's get into them.

Do not complain about poor sales

I said this once before, but it's another one of those things important enough to reiterate. It's okay to occasionally make a tongue-in-cheek post if sales are being wonky. I made a snarky meme video about sales once, and I have regretted it ever since. It's funny, but it's not professional. Complaining about book sales is not a smart thing to do in public because it tells readers that, for some reason, people don't want your book. That makes them think they don't want it, either.

Also, complaining about sales is not professional behavior. Ronan Harris of VNV Nation, one of my favorite musicians, gives 110% of his performance and energy whether he's playing to stadiums of thousands overseas in Germany or playing to an intimate goth club in Boston that holds maybe 300 people. He doesn't complain about fewer ticket sales in the U.S., and he celebrates the smaller venues just as hard.

Treat your writing the same when it comes to the public.

Behind closed doors, it's okay to express frustration, sadness, or all the other emotions to people in controlled spaces. Author groups are a safe place for that, usually. We get it. Selling books is hard, and it sucks sometimes to check your sales and see a flat line at zero. But don't share that side with your readers.

Don't tear down others

When I say "tear down," I mean engaging in drama. If there is a problematic author doing bad things you are calling out and speaking about, that's a different thing altogether, but engaging in squabbles or petty nonsense is not a good look. This includes doing things like tagging authors in reviews of books that you don't like, saying mean things in comments, or otherwise being venomous or backbiting.

If you are calling out someone doing something problematic (like many of us did with J.K. Rowling, for example), be direct about what the problem is, why you're taking a stand on it, and why it's important. Limit things like that to calling out actual problem actors, too. Don't just snarl at people for existing or writing a trope you don't like.

Don't reply to reviews unless it's thanking them or using them as marketing material

I get it. Bad reviews hurt. They really do. And it's never going to be easy or feel good to receive one no matter the source. It's even worse if someone misunderstood something or is acting in bad faith. However, don't respond to that hurt by lashing out, trying to clarify or course correct, or otherwise engage with the reviewer. Leave it alone. The review is what it is, and you howling about it will just make you look weaker.

If the review is left by someone who is not acting in good faith or who is salty about something that you can use as marketing (someone I know wrote a book on religion and uses negative reviews from bigoted folks as marketing material), go for it. But do this carefully and sparingly. Sometimes, it can feel good and be funny to grab a review like that and use it to your advantage, but more often than not, I advise against poking the bear. Just ignore it.

Deeply consider posts about political and social issues.

If you are going to weigh in on a specific political event, legal action, social issue, or other such thing on your public author social media, make sure you seriously think about what you have to say. Be articulate, eloquent, and thoughtful. I'm not going to be the person to tell you to not have opinions on political goings on, but I am going to tell you to think about it.

Sharing political memes, for example, should be a no-fly zone unless you're being very careful about it. Sometimes, a well-placed satirical comic can speak volumes. However, know that your political posts can easily be places where your fans will attack each other and you. It can become toxic and problematic very quickly, so make sure you engage in such topics with serious gravitas and awareness.

As authors, we should avoid reaching for the lowest common denominator of communication and work hard to live up to our status as wordsmiths. If you're going to talk about something on your public profiles, do so with the same level of thought and awareness that you would use to deliver a collegiate lecture. You don't need to write that volume, but give it that thought. And don't get into political arguments in public. You can make your stance and back yourself, particularly if it's important to you, but don't go starting X (Twitter) fights. It's not a good look.

Check your ego.

I have seen authors, plural, on more than one occasion get snarly with their readers as if their readers owe them their attention. As if they, the author, are someone important who *deserves* something from people. I'd like to say right now: Cut the crap. Coming across as self-important, selfish, and entitled regarding your interactions with others is a rapid-fire way to turn them on you.

Even as public figures, we are just humans. I am still just Ellis. My family is proud of me, but they don't think of me as some hotshot editor. I'm the kid who thought my family's hall closet was the bathroom late one night and got stuck in there when I was four, and my mom had to both rescue me and clean the floor. I'm still the sibling who accidentally ran my sister over with a horse. My friends view me as the weird gremlin they game with and laugh with and go to movies with. My husband just sees me as his partner who should probably catch up on folding laundry. I'm not different. And that's an *excellent* thing.

No matter what our skills or social status might be, we are still just people. We are not more important than or better than others. Heck, you, who's reading this? I'm not better than you. Different, maybe, with different knowledge and skills, but not intrinsically *better*. I'm still just a human being sitting in their PJs while I type this while drinking far too much soda.

Sticking yourself above others for most any reason—whether it's a traditional publishing deal, a certain success with sales, a certain level of knowledge or skill—is not a great way to make friends. Worse, it's a turn-off for people looking to connect with you. While, yes, it's okay to acknowledge and affirm your success and skill, you shouldn't view yourself as superior to others.

I bring this up because sometimes, the mere act of becoming a public figure sets off a power trip in certain people. Stay humble, stay human, and stay personable. It will get you much farther in life than if you become a self-important jerk.

What Not to Share in Public

While some of this was covered in the last section, there are definitely things you shouldn't share in public that are beyond the scope of my rules. These are, however, less clear-cut than the rules are, so I didn't want to give you a laundry list of them.

When we're posting on social media as our author selves, we need to remember that our potential audience is everyone who speaks the same language as us or whose computer has the ability to translate our words to the language they speak. In short, a huge swath of the *planet*.

I bring this up because we need to consider what we are okay with the entire world knowing about us. This is partially covered under the branding conversation, but I wanted to get into more depth here because there are a few things we need to think about when posting to the entire world.

The first thing I want to direct your attention to is personal safety. Authors of fiction may rarely end up on the list of people under serious threat from others, but personal safety is a reality. Don't share things that are geo-tagged unless it's a public event you're attending. Don't give out your home address to strangers on the internet. Use caution when discussing family members, particularly your kids who might not *want* to be famous. I'm not saying this to try and make you paranoid about everything, but use care when sharing that kind of information because it is public, and it can be used to do you harm or steal your identity if you're not careful.

Secondly, give serious thought to how much personal information you want to give to the entire world. It can be easy for some folks to over-share regarding personal details. Some authors have that as part of their brand. If you're doing things on purpose with full knowledge and intent, then you are making an informed decision. However, we need to make sure we are *making* that decision.

Be thoughtful when disclosing things like disability status, neurodivergence, gender, sexual orientation, financial status, or about a million other things. Whatever information you share about yourself, make sure you are intentional about the experience and don't just hand it out like Halloween candy.

Also, remember that when you choose to become a public figure, the anonymity of the internet wanes. The bigger you become, the more likely it is that people will really start looking for you and find things you say or find accounts you have or find places you talk, whether you really intended for that to be public or not.

Which brings me to my next point.

The Internet Remembers

While most people recognize that humans grow and change over time, the internet remembers. If you posted a lot of toxic or unpleasant things on an old LiveJournal account you thought you'd deleted, someone might connect that to you now and cause you a headache. Also, if you do nasty things now, people *will* remember.

Once a thing is online, it is very difficult to remove it. When things are out there in the public eye, you lose control over what people think of them, and of you. You can absolutely address something that comes up, but it's something you need to be aware of and prepared for. This is doubly and triply true if you post something awful.

Even among my own social circle, I know of someone who shared a bigoted meme, said some awful things under it when called out, and then deleted the post. Other people had taken screenshots of the post before it went down and of this individual's frankly awful responses. The person who had posted the thing posted an almost-apology, got called out for that with screenshots of what they'd actually said, and then deleted the almost-apology and lost friends for it.

I'm not saying that we should "cancel" everyone we disagree with. Don't get me wrong. The reason I bring up that story isn't to scare you from ever posting online. It's to make sure you're mindful and think things through before you hit "send" or "share" or "retweet." If you screw up, apologize and move on. You can't be perfect, and most folks accept apologies with grace.

Also, if you're acting in public spaces, too, people will notice. People on Facebook know my personal profile name, and that's the one I use when I'm interacting in writing spaces. If I say awful things, my author brand is connected to that account because I have links on my profile and so on. Also, it's not hard to figure out who I am if you look. I'm not exactly hiding.

How you behave has consequences, both good and bad, and the internet will remember just like a Telltale game how you behaved and made people feel. And screenshots are a very real thing to be aware of. If you post something controversial or upsetting, or if you're mean to someone, the internet *will* remember.

And the internet holds grudges.

Summary

Social media is an important tool, though not an entirely necessary one. Eschewing it is a decision you can make, but it will make marketing much more difficult and can require other, more costly, options. That said, using social media effectively does require a certain degree of social understanding as well as consistency in order to build and maintain your audience.

Key Takeaways

- Deciding which social media platform(s) to inhabit is a function of deciding which of them you enjoy the most and where your target audience is likely to be found. You do not need to be on all of them, though you should claim your author username even on platforms you do not intend to use.

- Social media is, first and foremost, social. Ensuring we do not stick our feet in our mouths and start chewing is necessary because public gaffes can be career-destroying if handled incorrectly.

- Adhere to basic etiquette or pay the price. Remember, what you say in public will be remembered, so don't do things like complain about sales, tear down other authors, or be unkind to people.

- Knowing what not to share is just as important as knowing what to share. Remember your target audience and share content that they would connect with rather than just anything that comes to mind. Your public social media face should be very separate from your private one!

- Use care and thought when handling things and when posting because even if you delete something after saying it, there is a chance that someone will have taken a screenshot. The internet remembers when you are a jerk, and it will keep receipts.

Chapter Fourteen

Advertising

Whole books could be, and have been, written about advertising. There isn't enough room in this book for that, but there is space to write to address fundamentals that you can use to build a foundation. From there, I suggest you seek out further information from other experts.

This segment of the book is intended to be an introduction to the concepts and give you a bit of a springboard so that, when you *do* talk to the experts, you can understand what they're saying more easily.

The Difference Between Marketing and Advertising

Much like how all squares are rectangles, but not all rectangles are squares, advertising is a part of marketing, but not all marketing is advertising. So what is the difference? This is one of the core mistakes I see people make when they start wanting to sell their book. They conflate the two and end up miserable and making no sales. These are the folks who drop book ads in every single writing group and then run off. It's sort of like cold calling, except you're cold calling the wrong people.

If marketing is, at its core, about developing relationships, then advertising is about letting the folks you have that relationship with know that you have a thing for them that they want. Marketing is a broad-scope concept that encompasses all the parts of letting people know who you are, establishing your brand, creating a sales funnel, and then using advertising to get people into said sales funnel.

A sales funnel, if you are unfamiliar with the term, is what it sounds like. It's the way you gather people who might be interested and draw them through the process of purchasing a product you have or whatever it is you're trying to get them to do. As a general rule, one of the major models used for a sales funnel is called AIDA.

- Awareness
- Interest
- Desire
- Action

There are other models out there. If you research "marketing models," you will find dozens if not hundreds of them that reflect different elements of marketing. That can, however, be overwhelming, so let's focus on AIDA for now.

The funnel begins with awareness. That's letting people know you exist and are a person or have a product they want to engage with. It's the first brush with you or your content. This might be an advertisement. It might be talking to you in a Facebook group. It might be seeing a TikTok video you've created. Whatever starts this funnel, they are aware you exist at this point.

Secondly, we generate interest. This is through multiple means, but the goal here is to make your customer actually desire the thing you have. This can also happen in that advertisement or content they see from you, but it can also be a slow development. With my editing, for example, people usually grow interested in working with me once they've talked to me about writing and editing and have discovered I know my stuff. Or they have watched enough of my TikTok videos and decide that yes, in fact, they are interested in what this gremlin in a teal bathrobe has to say.

Next is cultivating desire. This means you make them want the product. It is often a "hook" of some kind. It could also be someone going to your Amazon sales page and reading your blurb after realizing it's the kind of fiction they want.

Finally, you have action. This is the last step and is the customer taking the action you want them to take: buying your book, hiring you to edit, signing up for a course you teach, whatever it is.

That's the rough sketch of how it works. There's also a breakdown of when you are using AIDA for a specific advertisement versus how it works for an overall strategy. Think of that as funnels within the funnel.

Where the Funnel Breaks Down

You'll hear a lot of this sales funnel–type advice from expert marketers, and it's important to understand it, but there is something important we need to understand about it in terms of the writing industry specifically. The first piece is that marketing books is a different creature to marketing widgets. You can use a lot of the same concepts marketers use for other products, but we are inherently doing something a bit different.

The sales funnel idea is explicitly designed to market a single product or service. So, say, a class, a blanket, a cell phone. Books are different. They aren't exactly a single product because rarely is the book the only thing we're trying to sell. In order to be successful as an author, we have to sell *ourselves*. That means that creating these connections and developing this interest is more complex than AIDA when it comes to books.

Don't get me wrong here, AIDA is a valuable tool, and you shouldn't *ignore* conventional marketing advice entirely. We do, however, need to ensure this advice is viewed through the lens that some of what you'll find out there just plain doesn't apply to authors. The broad-strokes concepts of AIDA will work for us, but when you start digging into techniques for deploying it in marketing, authors often find it collapses since they're trying to sell the wrong thing the wrong way.

This comes with a caveat—AIDA works extremely well when applied to certain kinds of books, such as how-to and non-fiction works of a similar vein. It is, however, a *lot* more complicated when it comes to fiction and things like memoir.

AIDA focuses on finding a need and meeting that need. In fiction, we're not looking for needs, exactly. We're looking to amuse, entertain, inspire, and educate, but we aren't filling a specific *need* in the sense that we're not marketing to a person who is looking for a new widget. People are often perusing for books, but creating a *need* in them for that book is a lot more difficult. And that's where hooks come in, which we'll get into in the next section.

Advertising Principles

No matter where you look them up, you'll see different philosophies on the core principles of advertising. However, having read many of the websites and books, and gone to college to study business, I am going to break it down into five basic points that you'll need to consider when you approach advertising.

Honesty

I cannot stress this one enough. Be *honest* about your advertising. Don't use sex to sell your book if you aren't putting any in it. Don't claim to be a genre you're not. Don't use comparable works that are barely related. Don't shove your book in a category on Amazon that it doesn't belong in—to your best knowledge, anyway. Don't make promises or claims that aren't accurate.

Honesty is the foundation of developing trust, which is an absolute *need* in a business relationship. Once trust is damaged or shattered, it cannot be recovered. If your readers don't trust you to deliver what you say you're going to, they're not going to buy your books. Worse, they will probably leave angry reviews or tell people not to purchase your materials.

Brand Consistency

Your brand as an author is extremely important. Who readers know you as is going to shape your sales and shape what their expectations are. This isn't to say you can only write one genre or type of book, to be clear. You're allowed to experiment. But if you are Nora Roberts and known for your romance but also want to write thrillers, you might be better off with a pen name (J.D. Robb). Her pen name is an open secret, and she uses it to identify to readers that the books under each pen name are going to be *different*. Her J.D. Robb books are crime thrillers, whereas books written as Nora Roberts are romances.

While you don't need a different pen name for every genre, if you're writing things that very much don't fit together, like sweet romance and gritty crime thriller, you'll want to make sure there's a clear distinction between those categories.

This consistency also falls into things like font choices on marketing materials, perhaps choosing a logo, and considering a color palette. Creating visual consistency through your advertising will assist your readers in saying, "Oh, hey, I know that author. They're the one who wrote 'x.'"

Originality

Standing out from the crowd means leaning into the things that are uniquely you and your books. Yes, you might be writing in a crowded genre, so lean into the things that distinguish you from others. What makes your story different?

I'm not saying you need to be wholly unique here. But you'll want to think about the things your book has that others don't. These things will provide you options to help readers remember you and help them identify *you* versus others around you.

Simplicity

If your marketing funnel is overly complicated or long, people won't engage with it. Advertising operates on emotions, and you don't need to make things labyrinthine in order to be effective. When in doubt, go for the straightforward, direct solution if you can. You don't need all kinds of complex nonsense to make people want your books. There might be complexities on the backend (e.g., newsletter welcome automations can be a complex beastie), but on the reader end, you want things as clear and simple as possible.

Money Doesn't Fix Everything

For those who have it, there's sometimes the instinct to just keep throwing money at a problem. That might be increasing bids on Amazon or Facebook ads, or other such things if an ad is underperforming. Or it might be the instinct to just hire someone else to deal with all this and avoid it entirely. The reality is money does not solve all the problems you may encounter. You will have a lot of study and thinking to do to ensure you spend your money wisely.

Whether you are affluent or on the raw edge of not being able to make rent, money is going to be something in your mind because, when you're spending it on your marketing and advertising, you'll want to do so in the most advantageous manner possible. Dumping cash into an ineffective advertisement won't make it more effective, after all. Nor will hiring someone to market your books if you don't intend to do the work to give your publicist what they need.

Choosing Where to Advertise

Before we go too deep into this, I want to make clear that there's no one-size-fits-all for this. Every author, every genre, and every *book* will have different needs. You also are going to need to account for the fact that you will have platforms you connect with that are different than others who share the same genre and audience.

There is a lot of talk out there about this subject from folks with more experience than I have, but I do want to comment on the reality that this choice isn't just about metrics and data. Metrics and data *are* important and necessary. I won't try and say otherwise, but you also need to account for what you as a human connect with. If all the metrics and data say that your best platform is one that you absolutely do not want to be on, then don't be on it.

With that out of the way, you will discover there are about a billion places where you, as an author, can advertise, and they all want your money. From social media companies to Amazon to BookBub and other platforms, there are a lot of choices out there. Not to mention the people who will sidle up to you and ask if you want to promote with them. Don't do it; they're usually scammers.

So what do you do with all this?

Your first step is to assess where you are in your career. What works for someone who is selling more books than you are won't work for you necessarily because you are at different phases. It's kind of like how beginning writers have certain rules they abide by versus professionals who know the rules and decide when to break them. So where are you?

If you are at the very beginning of your career—which I assume you are if you purchased this book—you will want to focus on places that are low risk as you build your platform. For fiction authors, you also need to understand that you are likely not going to see a lot of sales and traction for your first novel. Building a platform and brand takes time, so at the outset of your career, you are going to want to invest most in places that will develop your platform.

What the heck does any of that mean? It means start small. Go grassroots with this process, and begin with things that aren't going to cost you a lot of money. Amazon ads are a good beginning, as is investing in your newsletter and building it. You will be able to advertise your book there without paying for ad space since, well, it's yours.

Paying for some advertising on social media focused on your target audience is also a good way to go. You can also try posting in some of the reading groups that allow promotion, but I have honestly never seen a single sale from those efforts. Most of those groups are populated by authors who swing through, drop a promotion, and never come back until their next book. Readers don't hang out in places where people are screaming "BUY MY STUFF" constantly. We get advertised enough everywhere else. I wouldn't go to a place that was just advertisement.

In Chapter 13: Finding Your Target Audience, we talked about finding readers, so knowing where your audience is will determine where you focus your advertising. You can also do a fair amount of advertising without spending money. Creating short-form video content and social media posts doesn't have to cost a lot of money, if any, and it can help connect you with those people.

I'm sure you've noticed I have mentioned very few specific places to advertise in this segment, and that is by design. My goal here is to provide evergreen advice. What platform(s) you choose to spend your advertising dollars on will change as we see new platforms come and go over time. As I write this, we are in yet another go-around of whether or not TikTok will continue existing in the United States, and we witnessed the collapse of X (Twitter). In the future, Amazon may not be the giant it is now, though I suspect that one is going to last for a while.

To summarize all this into a neat little package: Start small and grassroots with things that are low risk and don't cost a lot of money. As you grow, you can invest in bigger things like BookBub ads, Kirkus reviews, and investing more money into your social media advertising. However, until you hit that point in your career, don't beggar yourself. The temptation to hurl money at advertising and expecting that it will solve your sales is real, and it's something all entrepreneurial folks deal with. Advertising is important, but you are better off investing in smaller steps when you're early in your career.

Slow but steady is going to be your friend. That said, if you're made of money, there are a lot of folks you can hire who will give you a strong start. My website has a list of folks you can turn to for various products and services, and

I keep that updated as I get to know more people in the industry.

Graphic Design Principles for Advertising

This is going to be about as simple a breakdown as I can possibly give you because graphic design is its own entire industry, and there is no way I can give you enough to replace that education in a short sub-section in a book on publishing. However, there are a few important things I want to note to authors because they are issues I see pretty consistently, and I want to save you some of those difficulties.

Accessibility

Just like with fonts, this one is top of mind for me. So many authors and marketers in general create graphics without regard to accessibility, and when you consider accessibility, it improves your advertising graphics for literally everybody. What do I mean by this? The first I want to address is contrast. When you are creating graphics or videos with text, you need to make sure the text and background elements have strong contrast between text and background.

One of the ways you can do this is by using white text with a black outline when doing subtitles on your videos (you are doing subtitles, right?). Many short-form video platforms, or recording software designed for them such as CapCut, allow you to design your captions, and doing simple white text with a black border allows the text to stand out against bright backgrounds or dark ones. It creates a clear contrast and makes the content readable.

Now, you can do this technique with other colors of text, but remember that ensuring the text "pops" against the background allows people with vision difficulties to read it. It *also* helps folks who have good eyesight because it makes the text more visible and will catch their attention better. Everybody wins.

Another element of accessibility you want to consider is using alt text. Many platforms these days auto-generate alt-text for images. However, you can write your own for most of them. Providing alt text for images on your website, in your newsletter, etc., is a small gesture that can make a lot of difference for your audience, given how few people consider it.

The aforementioned captioning is also important. If you are doing short-form videos—or any video, really—providing captions is extremely helpful for a wide variety of people from those with hearing impairments to folks with ADHD. Also, if your audio is muffled or distorted in any way, it will help people understand what you're saying even if their hearing is perfect.

As I said, accessibility helps literally everyone.

Color and Branding

Color theory has a lot to do with branding, and you can say a lot about yourself and your brand by the colors you choose. I am not going to get too deep into what each of them mean here, but if you look up what people associate with various colors, you'll see what I mean. In addition to that, you can strike different tones and share pieces of your personality with the colors you choose. An author who writes sweet books might find a lot of mileage out of using softer colors and more "springtime" colors. By contrast, an author who writes horror may go with the classic black/red/yellow combination. Also, color can have gender things associated with it if that's something you want to relay.

You can also use these colors all the way through your brand, from your website to your social media to your author logo to your book covers. While people may not associate you with the color every time they see it, the power of color and branding cannot be overstated. For example, if I tell you to think of McDonald's, chances are their red/yellow arches come to mind. Wendy's is red and white. Nike is black and white. There are strong associations that you can create with all these pieces. If you want to take it a step further, there are people who use this kind of branding and aesthetic energy to create all their content on social media.

Now, I don't choose to do that. My social media content has whatever colors on it that it has because usually, I'm recording myself while I'm doing things in the real world, though you bet your biscuits that teal bathrobe I have is something people recognize. While one of my brand colors was never intended to be teal, it's sort of become a facet of what people know from me.

Font Choice

When we're talking graphic design, another thing you really want to think about is fonts. Font has a lot to say about personality when we are talking marketing. If you want an example of that, take a look at brand logos and the fonts they choose. You can also look at font choices on things like social media interfaces, program interfaces, and so on. Those are not random decisions; they are specific choices made by the parent company to convey certain things.

Also, as a nod to the accessibility discussion again, some fonts are easier to read than others, and not just for folks with dyslexia or eye difficulties. Choosing a font that is readable versus aesthetic is a balance you'll want to work on in your design. There are many, many guides out there that have a lot more depth and detail regarding fonts than I can provide here (there are whole books on the subject), so I encourage you to investigate the specifics of those choices through other means.

Image Quality

If you're using images in an advertisement, you want to make sure they are high-quality images. What I mean by that is, please don't use grainy, low-quality pictures blown up to pixelation. Not only is this not accessible, it's also *ugly*. If you need a specific guideline, I always start designing with images that are at 300 dpi resolution. 300 dpi is the standard for good-quality printing (it's what book covers require), and while you may need to save images at a lower resolution for the purposes of certain platforms and file sizes, if you start with large, good-quality images, the end result will always be superior.

If you are using cell phone photos you took yourself, you want to make sure the images are not blurry, that the contrast is solid, that the subject is clear, and that you didn't rely on things like digital zoom, which produces blurry, pixelated results. I won't get deep into the weeds of photography here because, like all the other elements of this subsection, it could be a book unto itself. For the purposes of covering the bases, though, focus on high-quality images at 300 dpi, and you will get yourself a lot farther than folks who don't. Also, make sure you have the commercial rights to those images; Google image search does not give you the right to use something commercially.

Copy Writing Principles

How many of us, by a show of hands, have howled to the sky because writing a book blurb or synopsis feels like death? Or that writing something on social media for the purposes of marketing feels like trying to write a foreign language?

That's because it is.

Copy writing is its own art form entirely separate from our skills as fiction authors. We are wholly and completely entering a new sphere. It requires a few specific principles in order to be successful. So what the hell is this? Copy writing is writing explicitly crafted and designed to catch attention and provoke a click, a sale, or an interaction of some kind. It's writing unique to marketing, though it has some crossover with spheres like journalism, where headlines use marketing copy heavily.

As with all the other elements in this chapter, I am providing you the basic ideas. You will need to do further research to hone your ability to do this, but it's extremely important and cannot be neglected.

The Purpose of Copy

The point of "copy" is to make someone engage with the content the copy is referring to. In order to do that, it needs to accomplish one primary goal: make the reader feel something. While, yes, all our writing is intended to make people have emotions—that's the point of *art* for crying out loud—marketing copy has to do it in a very condensed, focused way. That's why you see so many emotional words in marketing. *An exciting new novel by master author Neil Gaiman!* The word "exciting" tells you what you're getting. "Master author" hypes up the author by making you feel like you can trust the person to provide good quality.

These principles are both the same as prose and different. If I'm honest, one of the key differences in copy writing versus prose? In copy writing, you *tell* rather than *show*. That's one of the things that feels so awful for us authors. Copy writing in general goes against many of the rules we have ingrained into us when we are learning to write. It's all about exaggerated language, telling and not showing, and distilling things into the maximum emotional impact in a way that often feels "cheesy" to those of us who are more interested in telling stories.

That said, the discomfort we feel writing copy can be aided by the fact that writing copy is an entirely different sphere to our prose, so when we are writing copy, we must firmly have our "business professional" hat on rather than our "creative" hat. For most of us, the "business professional" hat chafes a little, but it is one of those evils we need to endure.

Copy Writing Basics

As I noted in the previous segment, writing copy is about making the reader feel something. As a result, you need to let go of a lot of the things you'd otherwise consider. That isn't to say copy is supposed to be dishonest—it isn't. If you promise something in marketing copy and don't deliver it in the book, you'll get angry readers.

An example of this is a book I purchased that promised me a steamy romance set in a particular time period in the vein of another piece of media that I was into. When I purchased the book, I was immediately and completely disappointed to find that the time period was barely window dressing, and even then, every single piece of information about the time period was wrong. I'm not talking about being salty that someone didn't have the right hat for that era; we're talking the equivalent of wearing blue jeans in the medieval period without time travel. I'm very forgiving about historical romances because the "historical" element of that is usually a feeling rather than historical accuracy, but it took me so far out of what I thought I was getting that it earned a low review from me.

When you're writing your copy, you need to make sure you are not setting expectations you don't meet. That's of vital importance.

However, you absolutely need to make the stakes feel like they're incredibly high (for most genres; cozy has different expectations) and really elevate the emotional punch. It's also a place to highlight tropes you include in your novel if you're writing in a genre where tropes are a vital part of your strategy, romance and erotica especially. To do this, you want to try and keep your blurbs short, tight, and to the point.

In *How to Write a Sizzling Synopsis*, Bryan Cohen talks extensively about ratcheting up the emotion in your words, simplifying the plot to only the pieces that will sell books, and keeping readers grabbed by the metaphorical throat through the process. I strongly advise that you go read that book after this one and absorb his wisdom on the subject.

As mentioned in the AIDA flow, you need to hit those pieces in your marketing copy. This is more than just the book blurb, though. Copy writing influences all your marketing. This includes things like what text you put on visual ads, your social media captions on marketing posts, your website copy, and so on. These are all pieces of copy designed to do one of two things: sell your book or build your brand.

Where to Use Copy

Copy writing includes anything you are putting together for the purpose of furthering your sales. Articles can be copy writing at times, though I advise against it as a general rule. The majority of text on your website is going to be copy. Captions on social media posts made from your official author accounts may or may not be copy, depending on what their goal is. If I'm writing something personal, I won't be using copy writing principles. If I'm writing something designed explicitly to sell someone something, it'll be copy writing.

Copy writing is mostly limited to advertising or spaces where the goal is specifically to gain a sale. Don't bring copy writing into a group talking about craft. Don't use copy writing when you're writing something personal to connect with your audience. Don't use it in blog posts unless the whole post is centered around making a sale, like an announcement of your book cover or something.

The thing people most often run into is not knowing when to slip into that mode and when to take it off. When you're talking to another human being for purposes of networking, you should be focused on *connection*, not sales. People know when they're speaking to a living billboard. I can tell when I go to a talk or watch a webinar or when I talk to someone if their goal is to convince me to purchase their service/product/whatever. If I am walking up to a vendor at a conference, I'm expecting that kind of exchange; that's a venue where it's absolutely appropriate. However, if I attend a seminar or webinar that is supposed to help me accomplish a thing, and the entire seminar or webinar is focused on selling me that product without giving me the information and underpinning what I was expecting, I am going to be pissed off.

It's the sort of feeling you get when you go to the movie theater and have to sit through a literal *half hour* of previews and advertising for products you didn't go to the theater to get and would like to watch the movie you paid to see, thanks. You know that feeling? That's the one.

Pointing back to the conversation about marketing versus advertising, you use copy when you're advertising. If you are marketing, there's a good chance that connection is going to be better achieved by just being a human being connecting with another one and not someone who is waiting to drop a link to their product.

Summary

Advertising and marketing are not the same thing! Advertising is part of marketing, but it's only a piece. That said, it is also very important to the success of your books. Knowing the principles of advertising puts you in a position to use advertising effectively as part of your marketing strategy overall. It also puts you in a place where you can find genuine success in book sales through these means rather than throwing a lot of money at ads that won't move your books.

Key Takeaways

- Understanding AIDA and the concept of a "sales funnel" will help you develop advertising that grabs potential readers and draws them into your books and series.

- When advertising, remember that you must be honest above all else. You are not trying to sell at all costs; you are trying to make genuine connection to the audience who wants your book.

- Staying consistent with your brand and identity is extremely important in advertising. It sets expectations with your readers, and those expectations are very important meet.

- Pouring money into advertising is like throwing money down a hole if you don't know what you're doing and aren't paying attention to the ROI (Return On Investment). Make sure you watch your ads and analyze them for effectiveness.

- Creating accessible advertising images and design choices is important not only because it connects with disabled people but because accessibility helps everybody. Making sure you use high-contrast colors will ensure your text remains readable against backgrounds, for example.

- Copy writing is its own art form and requires study separate from the craft of writing prose. Understanding the function and purpose of copy writing will allow you to better craft your advertisements and drive up engagement and visiblity.

Chapter Fifteen

Author Events

As authors, we are going to need to, at some point in our careers, attend events in that capacity. I don't just mean mingling or networking events, though there are a number of excellent books that cover the subject, but events where you are going to be either the focus of the event, or at the very least, the focus of attention for a portion of the event.

If you find these kinds of things stressful, this is going to be a challenge. It's not easy to be in public and "on." Being a public figure at these times is an entire thing, and this chapter aims to give you some tools you can put together in order to make the experience easier and to help you prepare for it overall.

While the preparations won't prevent difficulties or problems from ever taking place, they'll definitely help you avoid certain kinds of problems or know how to handle ones that do arise while you're in them. I can't account for everything you'll face, but I can absolutely give you the benefit of my experience and help you understand better what you'll want to work on developing in yourself.

Types of Author Events

As with all things in the world, there are many kinds of events you can attend as an author, and each of these types of events has a different code of conduct and expectation. What a book club will want out of you is very different than what you may be expected to do running a booth at a conference. Knowing this means you can step into different headspaces for these different situations and walk into them with better preparation. It can also help take some of the anxiety out since, if you know what to expect, there's less fear of the unknown to contend with.

While this is *not* an exhaustive list, here are a few of the different kinds of events you are most likely to run into as an author:

- Book club invitation
- Public reading or signing
- Vending at an event
- Speaking at a conference

There are many other possible events one could attend, but I think that list should be enough to get us started. I'm going to give a brief run through each of the events and what kinds of things you should expect from them. We will get deeper into what you might want to have ready for various things in the planning segment, but I want to at least touch on each of these before we start exploring them in more depth.

Book Club Invitation

Meeting with a book club is typically a small-scale and intimate event. Attending one is an opportunity to share more information about your book and your process, and these folks will be hungry for it. Chances are they have already read your book in advance of inviting you, and they are likely to have questions for you about things in the book. "What did you mean by..." "Did the symbolism for..." These are the sorts of things to expect from them.

A coordinator may give you a list of questions in advance or not, but you should probably brush up on the details of the book they read so you are ready to answer them when they start grilling you about the relationships between characters.

These are often more casual affairs, so you won't need formal dress. I'd go with something professional and on brand. If you forgive me for the reference, think "church clothes." I don't mean the kind of church where you wear extravagant clothing. Myself, I favor a button-down flannel or dress shirt and jeans. My fashion sense isn't yours, but that ought to give you a base to work from. However, when in doubt, you can ask the organizer for what they expect.

Public Reading or Signing

Often, these events take place at libraries or bookstores. You can expect to read a segment of your novel, which may be left to your discretion or requested by the organizer, and likely do a Q&A afterward. People attending the reading may or may not have read the book you are reading from, but they may have read other works by you. They also may be people off the street who are interested in meeting a local author, or a not-so-local author if you're lucky enough to do a tour.

Depending on the size of the reading and who puts it on, they may or may not have someone moderating a Q&A that happens, and there may be an expectation of doing a signing afterward. If you're at a bookstore, a signing is very likely since they are going to want to sell copies of the book. The bookstore will order your book and have it on hand to sell. Copies that you don't sell at the reading may go into circulation at the store, or you may need to take them home. A library may do a signing, but they will expect you to handle your own inventory and sales since libraries are civic services rather than for-profit enterprises.

The dress code is much the same as for a book club, though if you attend one doing a cosplay of a character from the book, there are many audiences who will enjoy such a thing. Depending on the venue and the audience, you may or may not get more mileage out of that. When in doubt, ask ahead of time.

Vending at an Event

If you are vending at an event—Comic Con, author convention, Renaissance faire, etc.—you likely are paying to attend the event as a seller. Most often, the only things the venue will provide are a table and maybe an EZ-Up or equivalent thereof if it's outside. And even then, that's not guaranteed. You will need to check what the requirements are and what your event expects of you.

Vending requires a lot of moving parts, and you'll want to prepare for that by looking at the checklist later on in the chapter. I am not going to detail all the things necessary in this spot, but know that vending comes with expectations of you having copies of your book, any merch, table coverings, decor, and a means to handle transactions: cash box with change, magnetic strip reader, etc.

Your dress code will vary depending on the event. Everything from casual to full cosplay can be expected, so you'll want to make sure you know what the event expectations are. If it's an event like RAVE (Readers and Authors Vegas Event), you aren't expected to dress a particular way, but if you're at a Renaissance faire, you are likely going to be expected to fit into the event by wearing appropriate clothing.

Speaking at a Conference

Being a speaker may or may not come with the ability to sell books at the event, and you may or may not have to manage that process. I've spoken at multiple events, and they run the gamut from having someone who will handle your books for you (with retail discount expectations) to not allowing you to sell things at all.

Conferences will all have set expectations as to whether or not you can mention your books (or services or whatever else) and will inform you in advance. If they don't give you that information in the literature in advance, you can always ask the organizers.

When speaking, you will likely be either on a panel with multiple people or speaking solo. The majority of conferences I have attended or spoken at have spots between forty-five minutes and an hour. As a rule, you are typically expected to have 10-15 minutes of that time, minimum, dedicated to Q&A from the audience. Depending on the type of talk and the conference, you may or may not need a slideshow presentation.

Dress for these events matches the expectations of the conference. If the conference is low-key, you can probably go in casual dress. I tend to like an excuse to dress up and default to a three-piece suit because I look dapper as hell, but you can always ask the conference organizer what their expectations are for speakers. Most often, they want business professional. This means a nice blouse or button-down, maybe a polo, and khakis or dress pants or a skirt. You're looking for the kinds of things you'd find in a lawyer's office. You don't need to wear a suit, of course, but cleaning up and looking good is strongly encouraged.

As an author, though, this might be something we do a little differently. I have a friend who does her talks in a highly polished latex gown and some others who do things in other eclectic gear. That's not a bad thing since authors are considered to be a little off-beat, but you'll want to consider your audience and your branding if you go that route. Make sure it's a choice *and* double-check with organizers to ensure you're within your guidelines of what they want at an event.

Planning for Author Events

This will look different depending on the event, but there are a few key questions you need to ask yourself as you are preparing. These questions will help you shape your approach. Also, this is not intended to be a full packing list (there's a checklist later in the chapter, though). The intent here is to help you get into the mindset and know what questions to ask so you can be prepared for what you'll require.

Let's take a look at the questions:

- Is this event physical or virtual?
- Do I need to bring my own books?

- What kind of location does the event take place in?
- Do I need to travel to attend this event?
- What am I doing at this event?

Is this event physical or virtual?

Preparing for a virtual event is different than preparing for an in-person appearance, obviously, but that doesn't mean there aren't preparations to put into place. You'll want to ensure your space and background are tidy, that you have nothing untoward visible, that your family or housemates are aware you are going to be unavailable, and you'll want to be somewhere quiet with good lighting.

Virtual events will require a stable internet connection, possibly a ring light or other lighting, and a decent-quality webcam. Overall, virtual events are less work than in-person ones, but they do have some up-front investments.

Physical events, conversely, have a lot of preparation associated with them from travel preparations, even if it's just a short drive, ensuring you are familiar with where you are going, packing the things you need to pack, etc. There's a lot that goes into them, so making sure you know which one you're going into will shape how you approach your pre-event time.

Do I need to bring my own books?

At some events like bookstore signings, the location may or may not require you to bring your own stock. This is, of course, assuming you're bringing books at all. Some events aren't about sales, and having copies of your books with you may not be what the venue requests.

If you are bringing your own books, you'll want to calculate how many you need and how many you're likely to sell. I was on a panel at a local library event where a bookstore was handling sales, but we needed to supply our own books. I brought five copies each of my books and went home with four of each. It wasn't a huge blow since attending the event at all was an honor. This kind of thing does happen and isn't a referendum on you. I was there to speak, not vend.

What kind of location is the event?

An outdoor event will be very different than an indoor one. Also, a comic con is very different from a library. The type of location the event is held in will give you a lot of information about what you'll need. A Renaissance faire, for example, may require you to bring your own setup entirely and often will not have tables, power, or running water for use. You may also need to bring some kind of shelter since standing in the sun all day will be detrimental to your health!

Knowing the location will also ensure you are prepared for some of the complications that can come with that. Back to the Renaissance faire: If you are in an open field with no power or running water, you'll need to be ready to use a portable toilet, which may inform your clothing choices, as well as ensuring you pack your drinking water, snacks, and so on. You might take a cooler and bring extra water, whereas in a convention hall, you have air conditioning. Also, outdoor venues have *weather*. You'll need to be prepared for nature do to its thing. Keeping an eye on the weather is more vital for an outdoor event than an indoor one.

Nobody wants soggy books.

Do I need to travel to attend this event?

Travel here means more than a drive around town. If you need to go a ways away or take a train or plane to get there, you'll need to factor in travel time and expenses. This might also mean shipping your books and the cost of transporting those things to the venue. Doing a comic convention a fifteen-minute drive away is an entirely different creature compared to doing a vending table halfway across the country.

If you're speaking but not selling books, your requirements for travel are likely to be less stringent. However, for us disabled folks, there are still considerations to be made regarding accessibility and our personal needs, such as factoring in the exhaustion of travel and time zone changes. I attended the final 20Books Vegas in 2023 as my first major author conference, and I arrived a full day early and left a day after the conference ended because I knew I would need the extra time to sort myself out and prepare for air travel. Not to mention meeting my needs as a disabled person and ensuring I was adequately rested if at all possible.

What am I doing at this event?

If I'm speaking only and not selling books, I can immediately cut out a portion of my preparations process. I don't need to pack table tents, decor, books, and so on. I can just show up, speak, and flee into the bog from whence I came. What you're going to be attending this event to do will shape what you need to bring. A networking event amongst authors will likely require business cards but little else, whereas selling at a convention comes with the requirements of a cash box, magnetic strip reader, inventory, and so on.

Knowing what you're at the event to do will give you a lot of mileage for planning as well as shape your expectations of what you can accomplish. If you're there to speak and *maybe* sell a book or two, you shouldn't expect to sell a hundred books. You won't need to bring the mother lode. If you're there to sell books but not speak, you won't need a PowerPoint prepared.

Ensuring you have a clear view of your intended activity at the event will ensure you have the physical items you need to be successful as well as being in a mindset that will be productive. If you go in expecting to sell a bunch of books at an event where sales is not the focus, you'll end up miserable and disappointed.

How to Be a Speaker

If you're speaking at an event, there's often a lot of anxiety that comes with that, particularly if you aren't a public speaker in other arenas in your life. That said, there are a few things you really do need to know about being a speaker at an event, and enacting these will save you anxiety as well as ensure you are following the social rules. Not to mention the event staff being grateful that you actually show up prepared!

The first thing you're going to want to know is *you are acting as a public figure.* While you are at that event, you are representing the event even when you're not on stage. That means you are expected to be "on." If you are at a multi-day event, this means in the evenings, you should not get extremely drunk and foolish anywhere where event attendees are likely to be involved. You also ought to comport yourself in a way that represents the event, and yourself, in a positive light. This doesn't mean that, if the event implodes, you need to apologize to attendees and do the job of organizers, but you ought to remain professional if at all possible.

Next, you will want to be prepared for your speaking slot early. That means not doing your slides at the last minute overnight the day before you present. It also means communicating with conference staff, arriving where you are supposed to be when you are supposed to be there, and being ready to go. People managing speakers are forever dealing with difficulties, and those running conferences have about a million irons in the fire at any given time. I say this as someone who runs one (the Neurodivergent Publishing Conference is my baby). If you are ready, polished, and know what you're doing and when you're doing it, you will be a huge asset to the organizers.

When preparing to be a speaker, you'll need to know if you're speaking solo or if you're on a panel. If you are speaking solo, you will want to prepare a talk that will last for the duration you are given with a little space for Q&A if possible. This means knowing how long your talk is going to take, ensuring you have it organized, knowing that you have slides with enough information on them, and practicing your talk if you aren't an experienced public speaker.

When I say "practicing your talk," I don't mean memorizing a speech like lines for a play; you'll likely have a set of bullet points that guide you through your talk and use those to cue you. If possible, have a clock somewhere so you can see where you are in your time, and make sure you are not over or under time. You can practice this at home until you get a good metric for it. It requires a little practice, but it's easier than you may think.

If you're on a panel, you'll want to make sure you know the panel topic. Often, you will get a list of questions in advance and can think about how you'd respond. While on a panel, you also need to recognize there are multiple people speaking, so try and keep your answers to the point if you are able to. Don't be terse about it, but try and ensure you are concise to respect the fact that others will also have replies to these questions, and you have limited time.

Also, while on a panel, be respectful and friendly to your other panelists if you are able to. If you're on a panel with people you *vehemently* disagree with, you can retain your politeness without sharing their opinions. Remember debate rules in those circumstances: attack ideas, not people. That said, I don't advise putting yourself in those situations if you can avoid it; it's exhausting. You may encounter them without warning, however, so be prepared to face such things.

During Q&A, you may have people cause difficulty. I mentioned earlier in the book the heckler I dealt with at the first in-person event I spoke at. He started off by threatening the editors on the panel, implying that we are the enemy of authors. The two people I was on the panel with didn't know how to reply to him. I defused the situation by both answering his question and making him look like an idiot. He was asking if we weren't scared for our lives, so I made eye contact with him, smiled, and said, "Nah. I know Kung Fu." It's both true and a funny pop culture reference. The crowd got a laugh, and I went on to answer the question, but I addressed it to the audience, not him. He tried to argue with me, but he was quickly shut down.

He didn't meet me in the parking lot, either.

The point I'm making here is that humor, refusal to rise to the bait, and confidence will go a long way to shutting down hecklers or troublemakers. Also, events typically have security, or the organizers will handle things like that themselves. However, I've spoken at multiple other events and in other locations, and that's the only actual heckler I've ever faced, so it's not a frequent risk in most places you are likely to be.

How to Fake It 'Til You Make It

As we well know, most of the time, authors are gremlins in bathrobes who don't want to be perceived by others. I say that as someone who is writing this in their fluffy bathrobe and who makes most of their social media content in said fluffy bathrobe because screw getting dressed.

Unfortunately, that gremlin status often doesn't translate into what people expect of public figures when they are meeting them at events. Unless being a weird gremlin is your entire brand, in which case... go ham.

That said, our aversion to being perceived is a real thing we need to account for and accommodate in our lives. Imposter syndrome runs rampant through the artistic communities, and we are typically shy about our achievements and don't want to be talked to. When you're at an event, you need to shed this cloak entirely and instead step into a space where you project confidence.

This may look different for many people. For myself, I'm a tabletop role-player of many, many years, so my default has been to create a "character" I can wear in those circumstances. It sounds more nefarious than it is—it's just the confident version of me I pretend to be when I am "on." Projecting confidence is a very different thing than feeling it, and appearance is what typically matters in situations when dealing with the general public.

If you are reading this and saying, "Okay, but how the hell do I *do* that?" I got'chu, boo. Don't worry.

Physical Confidence

The keys to projecting confidence have to do with body language and tone of voice. Using those cues on purpose will help a lot even if you feel like you'd much rather be anywhere else. The first thing to understand is that how you stand makes a huge difference. Carrying yourself with confidence may require some practice, so I'd give this a shot walking around Walmart or even in your own house. It'll feel awkward at first, but you'll start to settle into it in time.

Also, before we go *any* further, please understand that if your body will not do these things, you are not inherently unable to stand or move with confidence. I am physically disabled and cannot do all these things at all times. There are many elements to this, so do what you can where you can, and don't hurt yourself or despair because you have limitations. You can be disabled and still appear confident. I have Ehlers-Danlos Syndrome, ADHD, autism, CPTSD, POTS, and a whole lot of arthritis and tendinitis. You do not need to be able-bodied to employ what I'm about to teach.

Standing with confidence is largely something done in the shoulders. You'll want to straighten them up, which is uncomfortable, I know; many of us prefer to write while shrimp-shaped. If you are physically unable to stand straight for any number of reasons, do what you can without hurting yourself; this is not the only important thing. However, if at all possible, hold your shoulders back, upper back straight, and chin lifted a little. Don't overexaggerate it, but try and get yourself as close to "military posture" as possible. This body posture is associated with authority and strength. You don't need to be extremely stiff in this pose to be successful, either.

Another element of posture that can help is what you do with your legs. If you're standing, try and settle your weight into your heels with your feet shoulder-width apart, and plant yourself like a tree. If you are physically unable to do this, try and face the person you are addressing and keep the "planted like a tree" energy in whatever physical pose you have access to. This also works while sitting. Putting your weight straight down, if able, and keeping yourself erect with shoulders squared will give the same energy.

Talking about shoulders, also, try and drop them if you can. If your shoulders are hunched up to your ears, you'll look anxious and like you're trying to make yourself look smaller. Practice lowering them and feeling when they rise. This is, of course, predicated on your physical ability.

Walking with confidence is a function of all the above advice, plus walking with your hips leading if you are able. What I mean by that is it should be as if you have a string tied to your belt buckle, and that's what's tugging you forward. If you lead with your chest or head, it draws you over into that hunch I mentioned.

Vocal Confidence

Projecting confidence with your voice is another element you can engage. This can be done through tone but also through things like pitch and speed. I am coming at this from the perspective of someone who is a trained singer, so understand that what I'm talking about here is going to be related to that.

Let's start with speed. Speaking slower—not glacially, but with measured words—projects confidence, where speaking quickly can indicate anxiety. It can also indicate excitement, so if you're excited, you can absolutely show that, but practicing your speaking pace will help you appear more confident and more prepared. This is also true when giving a talk as a speaker or panelist. Also, speaking a little slower will help your audience retain your information and give them a chance to take notes.

Next, let's talk resonance. I think of all the vocal advice I can give you, this is one of the ones that will take the most work and the most intentional effort as it does change your voice when you do it. What I'm getting at here is speaking with your whole chest, just like with singing. It's not so much volume as it is richness. To do this, you'll want to focus on breathing with your belly rather than your chest.

In singing, we practice this by putting a hand on our belly and breathing. You should feel your hand move as your belly expands. If you're breathing exclusively with your chest, your chest will rise and fall, and your belly will be still. If you're breathing deep in your belly, your belly will move while your hand stays still.

Speaking from your belly and using that kind of breathing will allow you to project your voice further, increase the resonance, and improve the tone of your voice. It will also, by nature, make you louder. You don't need to use this technique all the time, but if you're public speaking or talking to a group, you may want to employ it. It also gives you a more "commanding" sound.

These two things alone will make you sound more confident and more settled in your own skin. Speaking a little slower and with more resonance will do a lot to project confidence to those listening. Also, bonus points, it's easier to speak with the resonance I described when your body posture is more erect and upright because, if you are all hunched in on yourself, you're putting pressure on your diaphragm, which makes it harder to do that belly breathing thing I mentioned.

Behavioral Confidence

The final piece is behaviors that project confidence. As an autistic person, I understand entirely how miserable eye contact is, but projecting confidence includes it. You don't need to constantly make eye contact with people, but meeting their gaze solidly at least a few times when conversing is important. It's a little silly that people make eye contact such a thing, but they do.

However, eye contact is not the only thing that helps.

Facing people when speaking to them, assuming it's relevant to do so, also helps. It's a body language thing, showing your attention is fully on them. This can have exceptions, such as when writing on a whiteboard during a lecture, or if you are stocking things or otherwise doing a task that requires you to focus on that, so don't force it to the detriment of what you're doing.

Remember, confidence is a collection of all these different pieces, not just any one thing at any given time.

Essentially, whatever it is you're doing, you want to project an air of, "I belong here." This is a technique that can get you a ton of mileage. Even if you feel like you don't think anyone would gain anything from what you have to say, don't feel like anyone would care about your book, would care about *you*. Acting as if you belong in a place and are among equals helps. This also includes speaking with people who are ahead of you in your career. Big authors, famous people... speak with them as if you belong speaking to them. That isn't to say to not be respectful—you absolutely should—but seeing them as just another human being in the same space you are and treating them as a human being you are excited to see is a valuable tool.

All these various techniques come together into the ability to put forward a confident, focused, knowledgeable front, even if your emotions are in the background screaming, "Don't perceive me!" A lot of these skills come down to acting. You are playing pretend.

When I am at an event and appear to be commanding a space or a room, or if I'm acting like I'm calm and relaxed and entirely in control, most of the time, it's a front. The thing you can also remember about this is that *most other people are feeling the same way you are*. The authors, artists, editors, and so on around you are frequently experiencing that same kind of anxiety around whether or not they're being seen.

The ability to project an air of confidence and calm takes practice, but you can absolutely make it happen, and it doesn't require that you wait until you *feel* like you're ready. If you wait until you feel confident to act as if you are, you are likely going to spend your life in waiting mode, and it will suck. Forge your way, friend. All the world's a stage and all that.

Event Preparation Checklist

This is going to have a few segments to it, and this is not an exhaustive list. It's a list designed for you to add onto as you find things you personally need. You also may not need everything I do on this list, so please make it your own. However, I know that having an actual list of items makes a huge difference to my anxiety, and having a template of how others do it helps me prepare.

Virtual Events

- Good-quality webcam
- Stable internet connection
- Good-quality mic
- Tidy environment to speak from
- Quiet space during the event
- Background free of inappropriate content or items
- Understanding of the platform you are presenting on or attending on
- Water bottle in arm's reach
- Good-quality lighting (ring light, natural light, whatever)
- Event schedule easily available
- Appropriate dress

In-Person Events

- Updated vaccines (particularly flu/COVID)
- Business cards
- Appropriate dress
- Insoles for your shoes (thank me later)
- Updated website and social media links on your site and/or business cards
- A small First Aid kit with Band-Aids, antibiotic ointment, pain medication (migraine meds, Tylenol, NSAIDs etc.), Moleskine, and any prescriptions you need
- A satchel, tote, backpack or other similar carry bag
- Notebook and pens
- Fully charged electronics (maybe chargers, depending on duration)
- Masks as needed depending on flu/COVID status in area, as well as allergens, etc.

- Chapstick
- Hand lotion
- Water bottle or container
- A small snack that requires no refrigeration (granola bar, trail mix, jerky, etc.)

Book Sales Events

- Table (may be provided by the venue)
- Table covering (can use a fitted sheet if you have nothing else)
- Marketing materials (bookmarks, tchotchkes, business cards, table tents)
- Books
- Cash box with change
- Card reader connected to purchase platform
- Inventory to sell
- Chair for you
- Chair for assistant (if relevant)
- Water and snacks behind the table; may require a cooler
- Electronic device chargers to ensure your card reader stays up and functional

If Outdoors

- Sunscreen
- Bug spray
- An extra layer if you end up cold
- Rain gear
- EZ-Up canopy or similar (if not provided)
- Tarp to cover books in case of rain
- Electrolyte additives or Gatorade (particularly if in warm climates)

- Battery pack for electronics

Travel Events

- Tickets for airfare or other travel
- Hotel reservations (if applicable)
- Arrangements for shipping books (if applicable)
- Toiletries and personal hygiene supplies
- Appropriate clothing for the climate and event
- Any medications needed during travel
- Travel items such as earplugs, neck pillow, or other comforts
- Look up where you can buy food or necessities local to the event
- Electronics and chargers
- N95 masks in case of traveling while sick

Final Thoughts

If you've read through this book and studied its contents, you should, I hope, now have a strong idea of what decisions you can make, what the steps are, and a path forward for your writing and publishing career.

This career path is not for the fainthearted. It comes with many difficult elements to it and can be very painful and stressful. However, I can also say I wouldn't want to do anything else with my life. For those who are like me—and if you're reading this, I suspect you are—publishing books and sharing stories with the world is almost more of a calling than merely a profession.

That said, if you end up deciding that this path is not for you, that isn't a failure. Writing is a labor of love, but selling it is an entirely different ballgame. There are many people who write millions of words on AO3 or Royal Road or Wattpad without ever trying to sell their writing. They write for the sheer joy of it, and I love that.

The only "failure" in this scenario would be to lose your passion for your writing. Whatever path you take from here, wherever your journey leads, my heart wishes you success. And if you need help? My website is a click away.

Summary

Author events are going to become something you want to consider doing as you develop your author career. While you don't need to start doing them immediately, they are going to be one of the things that really starts to gain you traction as your career progresses. Doing them has many considerations, but once you know what kind of event it is, where it is being held, and what you need to do to attend it, it becomes far simpler to plan for.

Key Takeaways

- Understanding the type of event can help you know what expectations will be on you for that event. Make sure you identify this in your planning stage so you know who your audience is.

- Planning for events means answering a few specific questions about what you will need and what you will be doing such as whether or not you will be vending, if you need to travel to attend, and what specifically you are doing at said event.

- Learning how to speak in public can feel intimidating or even downright threatening to most people. However, you can gain the skill and also learn how to project confidence and poise on stage even if you don't feel it. This takes practice, but you absolutely can do it.

- Congratulations! You have reached the end of this book. You are now prepared to take on the publishing world and triumph against the odds. Go forth and conquer, author friend. You've got this.

Want to learn more about publishing?

Receive your free self-publishing road map by signing up for the AUTHORiTEA newsletter. You'll also get regular updates with insights into the writing and publishing world from Ellis themself!

Scan me!

Or visit http://subscribepage.io/TheDamnBook

Acknowledgments

My journey into book publishing has been shaped by so many people. Far too many to name individually. I am grateful to the editors, authors, and people in my life who support my writing. You know who you are, and to name you would take up pages and pages because there are so dang many of you.

In addition to the people who have been with me through my publishing journey, I want to thank my family for their moral support, care, and encouragement. Particularly my mother, Linda, who has always encouraged my creative endeavors and who got me started on my love for books by reading me *The Hobbit* as one of my first chapter books. I can still remember her reading the opening lines of it as she tucked me into bed at night.

To my husband, Jason, who has been my loudest cheerleader and who has sacrificed much to share this writing journey with me. He has always been the first person to share my triumphs and my pains. I could not imagine a better partner.

I also want to thank my editor, Mel Ngai, who has helped me make my prose better and saved me from many embarrassing typos over the years. Cassiel Approves +10

Finally, I want to speak to all the writers reading this. You are why I wrote this book. You are why I do what I do as an editor. My heart and soul belong to the writing world, and I am ever honored that people choose me to walk with them on their journey. Working with authors is holding pieces of other people's souls in my hands, and I cherish that sacred space I am allowed into in ways too great for words.

www.ingramcontent.com/pod-product-compliance
Lightning Source LLC
Chambersburg PA
CBHW051821090426
42736CB00011B/1587